Studies in Global Justice

Volume 16

Aims and Scope

In today's world, national borders seem irrelevant when it comes to international crime and terrorism. Likewise, human rights, poverty, inequality, democracy, development, trade, bioethics, hunger, war and peace are all issues of global rather than national justice. The fact that mass demonstrations are organized whenever the world's governments and politicians gather to discuss such major international issues is testimony to a widespread appeal for justice around the world.

Discussions of global justice are not limited to the fields of political philosophy and political theory. In fact, research concerning global justice quite often requires an interdisciplinary approach. It involves aspects of ethics, law, human rights, international relations, sociology, economics, public health, and ecology.

Studies in Global Justice takes up that interdisciplinary perspective. The series brings together outstanding monographs and anthologies that deal with both basic normative theorizing and its institutional applications. The volumes in the series discuss such aspects of global justice as the scope of social justice, the moral significance of borders, global inequality and poverty, the justification and content of human rights, the aims and methods of development, global environmental justice, global bioethics, the global institutional order and the justice of intervention and war.

Volumes in this series will prove of great relevance to researchers, educators and students, as well as politicians, policymakers and government officials.

More information about this series at http://www.springer.com/series/6958

Michael Allen

Civil Disobedience in Global Perspective

Decency and Dissent over Borders, Inequities, and Government Secrecy

Springer

Michael Allen
Department of Philosophy
East Tennessee State University
Johnson City, TN, USA

ISSN 1871-0409 ISSN 1871-1456 (electronic)
Studies in Global Justice
ISBN 978-94-024-1162-1 ISBN 978-94-024-1164-5 (eBook)
DOI 10.1007/978-94-024-1164-5

Library of Congress Control Number: 2017945329

Printed on acid-free paper

This Springer imprint is published by Springer Nature
The registered company is Springer Science+Business Media B.V.
The registered company address is: Van Godewijckstraat 30, 3311 GX Dordrecht, The Netherlands

Contents

Chapter 1
Introduction: A Global Practice of Civil Disobedience

Abstract This introductory chapter, I lay out the idea of a global perspective on civil disobedience by appeal to Rawls' *Law of Peoples*. Indeed, I argue for an extension of the theory of civil disobedience from the peoples of liberal-democratic nation states to the international community of decent peoples. Here, the international standard of decency replaces the principles of liberal social justice as justification for diverse cosmopolitan citizens and states disobeying domestic or international law. Decency thus lays the foundation for a global practice of civil disobedience. The chapter offers brief discussions of the three cases of such a disobedient practice that I take up in detail in the subsequent chapters, along with the different issue that they raise for global justice. It also lays out my general approach to civil disobedience in a global perspective. I stress both the limits of liberal theory in light of diverse conceptions of justice capable of supporting a global disobedience practice, and the *positive contribution* of non-liberal viewpoints to advancing important global justice causes.

1.1 Introduction

In this monograph, I explore a hitherto unexamined possibility of justifiable disobedience opened up by Rawls' *Law of Peoples* (2001). This is the possibility of disobedience justified by appeal to standards of decency that are shared by peoples who do not otherwise share commitments to the same principles of justice, and whose societies are organized according to very different basic social institutions. Justified by appeal to shared decency standards, such disobedience undertaken by either state or non-state actors would challenge injustices in the international system of states. Rawls himself do not consider such a possibility of disobedience. Indeed, Rawls limits his discussion of civil disobedience in *Theory of Justice* (1971) to actions undertaken by the citizens of liberal states that are also, at least, minimally democratic. In this respect, he appeals specifically to the premises of

M. Allen, *Civil Disobedience in Global Perspective*,
Studies in Global Justice 16, DOI 10.1007/978-94-024-1164-5_1

liberalism, such as the moral equality of persons as free and equal citizens, along with majoritarian democratic mechanisms, such as 'one person, one vote.' Nevertheless, peoples worldwide do not share these liberal and democratic premises, as Rawls forthrightly acknowledges in *Law of Peoples*.

I want to argue that grounding civil disobedience in the *Law of Peoples* is a coherent possibility of justifiable political dissent in the international arena. This, however, is a possibility of justifiable dissent that entails detaching the moral right to disobey from its familiar moorings in liberalism and democracy. Such a possibility is one of considerable importance for achieving international or global justice. Indeed, urgent cases of injustices crossing the territorial boundaries of states that may be appropriately addressed through justifiable disobedient acts. These cases include (1) the plight of undocumented migrants; (2) the unfairness of international trade rules for the poorest and least powerful countries of the world; (3) the threat posed to international order and stability by government secrecy. In each of these cases, the moral right to disobey is defensible quite independently of the premises of liberalism and democracy. To be sure, it is also defensible in terms of these premises. Moreover, a defense given in these terms would be more compelling to the peoples of liberal-democratic states.

Nevertheless, the global scope of civil disobedience depends on grounding it in a standard appealing to peoples whose fundamental commitments to justice are neither liberal nor democratic. At any rate, this follows as long as global politics constitutes a system of peoples and states (Beitz 2011; Miller 2012; Nagel 2005) not all of whom are committed to the premises of liberal-democracy. In what follows, I first consider the idea of decency from the Law of Peoples as offering an alternative to the dichotomy of domestic social justice and international justice in Rawls' earlier *Theory of Justice* (1971). I then consider it as potentially grounding shared practices of disobedience, uptake, and reconsideration beyond the liberal-democratic state, in the cases (1) – (3) above.

1.2 Decency as a Shared Standard of Global Justice

Here, I turn to Rawls' concept of decency. Some political philosophers malign this concept as representing only a commitment of sovereign peoples to an unduly minimalist conception of human rights (for example, Buchanan 2007). These minimalist contents, for instance, include, without being limited to, international legal guarantees against servitude and guarantees of the satisfaction of subsistence need (Rawls 2001). Nonetheless, the decency concept also has its defenders, who emphasize that it is not solely about commitment to minimal standards. Instead, its normative significance resides in the role human rights play in an ongoing discourse between states and sovereign peoples on matters of international concern (Beitz 2011). On this latter view – which is indeed much closer to the one that I endorse – decency entails a commitment to maintaining such a global discourse, across fundamental differences concerning the particular contents and entailments of justice. Sovereign peoples are, as such, decent both in respect of their agreement upon certain minimal contents for human rights and in respect of their agreement upon maintaining a global discourse in which the contents of such rights may undergo revision and expansion over time (Ibid).

For my purposes in this monograph, the primary minimal content of human rights is the international guarantee of access to the basic elements of the rule of law. Why is this so? I believe the answer should be reasonably obvious. To be sure, civil disobedience campaigns may take forms not tied to claiming equal fundamental rights, as in some cases of environmental disobedience (for example, Welchman 2001; von Essen 2017). Nevertheless, historically speaking, disobedience campaigns have been concerned primarily with such struggles for equality of fundamental rights, entailing access to the rule of law. They have been about gaining access to basic elements of the rule of law, such as the ability to seek appropriate redress for grievances, openly contesting whether legal processes are in conformity with shared conceptions of justice, and demanding public justifications for coercive law and policy, without fear of reprisals (Beitz 2011; Rawls 2001).

Nonetheless, civil disobedience campaigns aiming to win equal fundamental rights of effective legal redress and ongoing contestation for the subjects of law typically appeal to domestic, as opposed to international, justice. Indeed, all of the most influential discussions of civil disobedience in the Anglo-American philosophical tradition have been so deeply rooted in the nation state (Bentouhami 2007), and its requirements of domestic social justice between co-national citizens, that its international implications have been obscured from view. Perhaps the most influential discussion in this tradition is that of Rawls himself not in his *Law of Peoples* (2001) but his *Theory of Justice* (1971). In *Theory*, Rawls embeds his account of civil disobedience in a theory of domestic social justice for an imperfectly, but nearly, just liberal-democratic society. Rawls conceives of such a society abstractly as an association of co-national citizens entered into at birth and exited only at death (Rawls 2005). This remarkably high level of abstraction in the conception of the state and its people is justified by Rawls as an analytical convenience, demarcating the domain of domestic social justice from questions of justice between different national peoples organized in different territorial states, in the domain of international relations (1971, 2001).

With this analytical distinction between domestic and international justice, Rawls effectively disengages from any consideration of the international scope of civil disobedience. He considers such disobedience only in the context of relations between a co-national people committed to specifically liberal principles of justice, insisting upon the equal moral status of persons, as free and equal citizens, who enjoy equal access to majoritarian democratic institutions. Indeed, when he turns to international relations of justice in *Law of Peoples* (2001), he makes no mention of civil disobedience whatsoever. His silence regarding its international scope is perhaps surprising when viewed in a historical perspective. After all, civil disobedience emerged historically from international contexts of politics. Henry David Thoreau's civil disobedience was in response to a war between the United States and Mexico (1993). Thoreau refused to pay the state poll tax implemented by the US government to prosecute its war with Mexico and enforce the Fugitive Slave Law. His concerns were clearly international in scope insofar as he saw Mexico as "unjustly overrun and conquered by a foreign army" as a means to expand the slave territory. Likewise, resistance to imperial rule motivated the Boston Tea Party. The same holds for Mohandas Gandhi's (1932) civil disobedience campaigns in South Africa and India questioning the standing of subordinate peoples in the British Empire. Gandhi's disobedience campaigns were, again, international in scope appealing not only to the conscience of imperial policy-makers but also to diverse publics at the peripheries and center of Empire. Nevertheless, these campaigns also appealed to the national publics of other countries, such as the United States, which Gandhi believe could be moved to become a powerful critic of unjust British imperial rule.

Nonetheless, Rawls' analytically convenient distinction between domestic and international justice made sense for him, given his particular focus on disobedience in the context of the American Civil Rights movement. After all, Black Americans denied equal civil and political rights by the White majority were US co-nationals. Moreover, the White majority were avowed constitutionalists committed to the moral equality of persons – "We hold these truths to be self-evident, all men are created equal ..." Disobedient public address was exclusively between co-national citizens addressing the majority about racial segregation laws that fundamentally disrespected liberal constitutionalist ideals. It did not engage policy or law at the level of any international global governance institutions, remaining focused solely on domestic US policy and law and domestic US governance institutions. To the extent disobedience in the context of the US Civil Rights movement appealed to human rights *as* civil and political rights, it did so only insofar as human rights ought to be protected and enforced under the national constitution of the US state. To be sure, the disobedience campaigns of Martin Luther King, for instance, did address a global audience. King's intention was, in part, to shame America in the eyes of the world (Corlett 2003). But, even so, it was certainly not a global audience that was invited by US disobedients to reconsider or reject domestic US policy or law; not, at any rate, in the sense of effecting a change of any internal, domestic arrangements in the US. Indeed, US co-nationals saw changes to domestic policy or law, above all, as their right and responsibility.

At this point, however, Rawls' analytical convenience begins to appear increasingly indefensible. It is undeniable that civil disobedients have long appealed to the conscience of a people, or many peoples organized in territorial states, to take action of some kind challenging fundamental injustices. Nevertheless, these might not be injustices suffered by the citizens of the state called upon to take some appropriate action. The victims of injustice may fall under the jurisdiction of another state, as in the case of undocumented migrants. Alternatively, they may fall under the jurisdiction of the community of states that has reached agreements on international term of cooperation that are distinctly unfair to some of its members. Here, the victims may be national peoples unable to exert power and influence over the formulation of these terms. Further, the victims might even be persons or peoples denied access to information vital to their ability to claim the status of moral equals, at the heart of the Rawlsian conception of decency.

1.3 Decency as Grounding a Global Practice of Civil Disobedience

I ask, then, whether decency may ground disobedient protests regarding these kinds of injustices, as explored in this monograph. An immediate objection to this proposition is that Rawls restricts the scope of civil disobedience to the citizens of the liberal-democratic state for a perfectly good reason. This is that relations of justice binding disobedients and their addressees are unique to co-nationals of such a state. In other words, there is no basis for such relations between co-nationals and non-nationals or between different peoples. Nevertheless, relations and duties embedded in a national practice of justice are hardly exhaustive of the obligations of justice. There are, at least, two ways to conceive of obligations beyond co-nationality relations; that is, two ways of conceive of obligations to the rest of humanity. According to one highly influential view, common features of humanity ground obligations to humanity as a whole (for example, Griffin

2008). This view is consistent with the *Law of Peoples* to the extent all of humanity have common urgent needs and interests in security, subsistence, and so on. It is not, however, consistent with the particular interpretation I endorse in this monograph of the *Law of Peoples* as establishing a global discourse of decency in which diverse kinds of global actors hold one another to account through a shared set of commitments. This interpretation does not dismiss the idea of common humanity (Risse 2015), but instead appeals to globalization as having established a system of rules constituting a global order in which relations of justice now obtain between all persons and peoples (Beitz 2008).

Either way, however, national borders do not limit the scope of justice. Nevertheless, both conceptions of obligations beyond the narrow confines of the state present difficulties for civil disobedience in global perspective. As non-relational, the common humanity view would appear to be fatal to this purpose. After all, civil disobedience presupposes that specific relations and duties should obtain between disobedients and their addressees. At a minimum, they must see each other as bound together in a shared practice of disobedience, uptake, and reconsideration. Consequently, appealing to shared discursive commitments, such practice-based relations of justice offer the best way to realize obligations to common humanity (see Caney 2006, for a cosmopolitan view of the priority of practice for realizing non-relational obligations of justice). That said, however, the second view is obviously less problematic. As relational, it can more easily accommodate the requirement for a global practice of civil disobedience. That is, it can more easily accommodate a practice of diverse actors on the international stage discursively binding different peoples to uptake and reconsideration, in light of shared commitments to realizing urgent human rights. Indeed, such a global discourse of decency lays the foundation for a global perspective on civil disobedience in at least three respects.

A global decency discourse may (1) take a global *intra*-state perspective on the practice of disobedience, uptake, and reconsideration among co-nationals. Nevertheless, it may (2) also take an *intra*-state perspective on such a practice obtaining instead between co-nationals and non-nationals, such as global migrants. Alternatively, it may (3) take a global *inter*-state perspective on a practice of disobedience, uptake and reconsideration between different peoples. In each of these cases, the primary subject of disobedient public address is peoples organized into states. Moreover, the decency standard of the Law of Peoples does the heavy lifting with respect to justifying disobedience. With respect to (1), the global practice of civil disobedience would mean that all peoples recognize the right of their own citizens to disobey domestic law and policy, when popular expressions of internal sovereignty violate decency. Citizens from each sovereign state would resort to disobedient protest, making claims of justice binding their co-nationals to uptake and reconsideration. Here, the global perspective would be one of many different self-contained societies, each providing its national citizen-disobedients with grounds for making such claims. That is, each self-contained society would provide its own citizens with grounds for disobedience and uptake in light of relations specific to their internal domestic arrangements.

Nevertheless, this first perspective continues to rely on relations and duties obtaining only between co-nationals. This is not to say that the intra-state perspective on disobedient public address and uptake between co-nationals is identical to Rawls' framework in *Theory* (1971), concerned exclusively with the liberal-democratic state. On the contrary, it departs from this framework in, at least, one vitally important respect. Appealing to conditions of decency (Rawls 2001), civil disobedients may be citizens of traditional-hierarchical, as well as liberal-democratic, societies. To this extent, co-national relations of disobedience, uptake, and reconsideration are no longer restricted to liberal-democracies. Nevertheless, this perspective alone does not take civil disobedience beyond the confines of the national state. Instead, it entails practices of civil disobedience obtaining worldwide within different kinds of states, among different kinds of peoples. Consequently, despite this worldwide scope, it remains consistent with *Theory* in conceiving of civil disobedience in terms of relations of justice exclusive to states and membership of states.

This continued focus on intra-state disobedience relations among co-nationals, however, is of limited interest to me in the following chapters. Indeed, such intra-state relations should remain the concern of co-nationals, as long as their relations to non-nationals conform to decency standards. This is a requirement of respect for peoples' autonomy and right to decide their futures for themselves (Beitz 2011). By contrast, the cases that concern me are those in which relations of disobedience, uptake, and reconsideration obtain between co-nationals and non-nationals or between different national peoples. These are cases falling under the (2) and (3) categories above. The first of these cases – global undocumented migrants – falls under the (2) category: an intra-state practice of disobedience emerges between the co-national people and non-nationals as global undocumented migrants. One of the impacts of globalization has been the migration of persons between states. This creates a circumstance different from that theorized by Hannah Arendt (2000) of *stateless* persons who are owed, by the international community, the right to have rights, where this, more often than not, is thought to entail membership of a state.

Instead, globalization has produced the problem of *undocumented* persons who are members of states, and indeed states that may well satisfy the minimal human rights standards of decency. But such persons – who are, by no means stateless – are driven by economic pressures to pursue opportunities in other countries whose borders they cross without inspection, authorization or permission, from peoples claiming sovereign control over their national territorial jurisdictions. This poses an especially difficult problem for a Law of Peoples that assigns normative priority (Risse 2015) to states and peoples. After all, the presence of undocumented populations within their territorial borders inevitably poses a challenge to their exclusive powers of internal sovereignty. Undocumented migrants violate the sovereign right of peoples to control their own borders. Nevertheless, the circumstances under which they live in the country whose borders they have crossed violate decency. These circumstances violate decency to the extent the undocumented have no effective guarantee of access to basic elements of the rule of law when seeking protection against harassment, persecution and domination by citizens.

Can, then, undocumented migrants legitimately take on the role of non-national disobedients binding the people whose laws they have broken in crossing borders and continue to break in working without papers, driving without licenses, etc., under an obligation of uptake and reconsideration? If so, then a very different global perspective on civil disobedience is established, one that does indeed go beyond the confines of the national state. As I argue in the subsequent two chapters, such a perspective would entail a practice-based relation of justice not simply between co-nationals within state borders, but rather *co-nationals and non-nationals* within these borders. Here, non-national disobedients would appeal to the decency of sovereign peoples to recognize and protect their urgent human right to effective legal protections against persecution and domination in the country whose borders they have crossed illegally. In this respect, decency becomes the ground on which undocumented non-national disobedients call for sovereign peoples to create domestic conditions of non-domination in the country in which they do not necessary have a right to stay.

This second intra-state perspective on a relation of disobedience, uptake, and reconsideration obtaining between co-nationals and non-nations also potentially differs from the first perspective in that the appeal to decency entails an expansion of the minimal list of urgent human rights in *Law of Peoples*. Disobedience between co-nationals could proceed without challenging this minimal list. Co-nationals recognize one another's right to be political participants in determining fair terms of domestic social cooperation, according to shared principles of justice. Nevertheless, such rights of political participation in domestic politics do not extend to non-nationals. I argue, however, for recognizing that undocumented migrants as legitimate participants in shaping the terms of domestic cooperation in those societies they have entered illegally and in which they have no right to stay. Indeed, the relation of disobedience, uptake and, reconsideration between co-nationals and non-nationals, implies a novel kind of urgent human right: the right of free and equal persons to be political participants, wherever they are.

Such a novel human right of persons is not restricted to disobedience by global undocumented migrants. For instance, multinational coalitions of like-minded persons – cosmopolitan citizens – may engage in global forms disobedient public address to the community of peoples as a whole. Here, cosmopolitan citizens engage with peoples not over the terms of domestic but rather global or international justice. They do so by protesting the incomplete or nearly just character of global, as opposed to domestic, arrangements. This phenomenon of disobedience often consists of challenges to unfairness in the present terms of global economic cooperation. Underwritten by decency, disobedience of this sort coordinates the activism of persons who are the citizens of both liberal-democratic and traditional-hierarchical societies. Global disobedient public address by cosmopolitan citizens, again, goes beyond the confinement of disobedience relations within different self-contained societies. Nevertheless, challenges to injustices in the terms of global economic cooperation are not limited to the activism of cosmopolitan citizens.

Indeed, *states themselves* may also take on the disobedient role by representing the moral character and conscience of their peoples in the international arena before other states representing other peoples (Kokaz 2005; Goodin 2005; Allen 2011a, b). This establishes the third global perspective on civil disobedience: an *inter*-state practice of disobedience, uptake, and reconsideration between different peoples. If states can legitimately take on this role, then shared, international practices, binding different peoples as related by their commitments to decency again realize global justice. Here, global economic inequalities between peoples do not point the need for a new human right of persons as global political participants. Instead, it exposes inequalities of rich and poor peoples to achieve sovereign self-determination: that is, inequalities in the capacities of different peoples, and not persons, to be effective participants in the global arena. Indeed, as I shall argue, the failure of decency is a failure to ensure a fair value of liberty for self-determining peoples in the global economic system. Grounded in decency, practice-based relations of justice between peoples potentially justify inter-state civil disobedience regarding unfair terms of global economic cooperation. Such disobedience-relations aim to realize one of the fundamental goals of the *Law of Peoples* in the fundamental equality of peoples and the *fair value* of their equal liberty qua peoples.

Disobedience by states, however, can also take a different and more ambivalent form. States may resort to illegal or extra-legal action not to challenge global economic inequities, but rather to preserve the conditions of decency and human rights for peoples. Here, I have in mind the idea historically defended by John Locke of executive prerogative in which the state acts independently of legal mandates, and sometimes even contrary to law, under certain kinds of emergency situations. Resort to prerogative accelerated after the terrorist attacks of 9/11 as governments increased their use of secretive surveillance programs, such as the mining of citizens' meta-data. Prerogative is ambivalent from the perspective of decency, notwithstanding its defensibility as necessary to preserve security of life and limb. Secretive uses of government prerogative violate the decency requirement for the publicity of government decisions. To this extent, they also preclude any possibility of citizens' gaining effective access to the rule of law by dissenting from decisions they believe violate their fundamental moral rights as persons.

Consequently, secrecy in the government's use of its prerogative power gives rise to yet another form of disobedience, not by states but rather persons with access to government secrets who elect to disclose those secrets to the public. Here, 'disobedient disclosers' have an equal claim to justification in resorting to discretionary extra-legal action by virtue of the non-publicity of governments in resorting to the secretive uses of prerogative. The upshot, then, is that governments and disclosers make competing and contradictory claims to be justified in going beyond the mandates of existing law. It is unclear, however, that this dilemma can be resolved by appeal to yet another addition to the minimalist list of urgent human rights in *Law of Peoples*, such as an urgent human right to government transparency. That, after all, would validate one justifiable claim to decency while contradicting another. Rather than a human right to global government transparency, decency thus requires the protection of diverse and sometimes contradictory disobedient actions. Such protection, however, does not entail immunity from legal consequences for disobeying the law or going beyond its mandates. Instead, it points more to a human right to leniency. State officials and disclosers may claim a right insofar as decency underwrites different and contradictory interpretations of what it may rightly prescribe. Here, leniency for officials and disclosers is justifiable as a response by reasonable peoples the irreducible complexity of politics.

1.4 The Approach

Overall, the approach I take to a global perspective on civil disobedience appeals to a related set of precepts and ideas.

1. That globalization has resulted in a global system of cooperation among persons and peoples.
2. That the global system is only near (Rawls 1971) or piecewise (Sabl 2003) just.
3. That states and peoples retain normative priority within this system for the implementation of decency standards and human rights.
4. That decency is a moral consideration capable of overriding the duty to obey either domestic or international law.
5. That such a duty may be defeated in cases of both justifiable intra- and inter-state civil disobedience
6. That global civil disobedients may be either persons or peoples.

In all these respects, the global perspective on civil disobedience remains consistent with civil disobedience as conceived by Rawls in *Theory of Justice* (1971). In other words, it remains consistent with the state-centered form of civil disobedience insofar as civil disobedience addresses systematic injustice or unfairness in cooperation between moral equals. Here, disobedients address a people who is ultimately responsible for making changes in domestic law and policy. That is, disobedients address the people who authorize their state as the complex of institutional arrangements embodying its shared conception of justice and collective moral character. In the global perspective, however, the difference is that disobedients address the international community of peoples as a whole. Here, the community of peoples is collectively responsible for guaranteeing orderliness and fair terms of cooperation in the global system. Nevertheless, civil disobedience plays an essentially similar role in highlighting the near (Rawls 1971) or piecewise (Sabl 2003) character of justice.

Indeed, a central idea of Rawlsian civil disobedience is that the domestic system of cooperation is not in complete *disorder*. Hence, civil disobedience applies only in a piecewise condition of justice in which there are functional institutions of law and justice. In Rawls' case of Jim Crow laws racially discriminating against Black Americans in the 1950s, for instance, the US people reliably administered justice for most but not all fellow co-nationals within its territorial jurisdiction. The global system is in a similar condition of piecewise justice to the extent there is a function system of networked global institutions, establishing terms of international cooperation (Beitz 2011). Moreover, this system is primarily the outcome of international treaty-based agreements between peoples and states (Ibid). Nevertheless, these terms of cooperation are only piecewise just (Ogunye 2015): the international community reliably administers global justice for only some but not all persons and peoples.

Consequently, it is the piecewise condition of justice in the global system that gives rise to the possibility of justifiable civil disobedience in a global perspective. In the Jim Crow case of piecewise justice and unfairness in the domestic system of cooperation, Rawls stressed that the piecewise failure of justice consisted primarily in the violation of political liberty rights (1971). For instance, Black Americans in the 1950s suffered economically from racial segregation laws. Nevertheless, the principal injustice or unfairness done to them was not that the economic inequities between Black and White Americans, but rather the denial of institutional opportunities for the former to be effective political participants in shaping the rules of cooperation. Civil disobedience, in the Rawlsian framework, thus took the view that any resolution of the piecewise order of justice required a fundamental reordering of the system of cooperation in order to guarantee the fair value of political participation.

Indeed, this meant, among other things, that civil disobedience was not justified by advocacy for any specific changes in law or policy – concerning, say, economic equity or border controls – beside those necessary to guarantee effective participation rights. Instead, participants work out specific policy proposals to address other injustices – such as distributive equity or immigration – through normal politics. That is, they work out responses to these other injustices in a reformed condition of society in which all can effectively shape public decisions, without resorting to disobedience. I appeal to the same priority on political participation, as the remedy to other injustices, for the global perspective on civil disobedience. Hence, in my first case concerning the undocumented, I do not ground justifiable disobedience in claims about the moral arbitrariness of borders (Carens 1987), or concerns about global economic inequities driving illegal border crossings. Instead, I focus on the lack of opportunities for undocumented migrants to be effective political participants in domestic politics wherever they are, appropriately shaping how a people's sovereign immigration policies affect their life prospects. Likewise, in the second case concerning global economic inequities, I focus not on such inequities per se but the lack of opportunities for the global poor to participate effectively in shaping the terms of ongoing economic cooperation.

In other words, the global perspective retains a Rawlsian focus on disobedience as highlighting unfair terms of cooperation – either domestically or internationally – in which not all participants have an appropriate and effective political voice. This, however, requires me to provide an interpretation of decency, in light of the priority of political participation for overcoming unfairness in cooperation and creating orderliness of the global system. To this extent, I am less interested in those aspects of international decency that commit peoples to meeting basic human needs for adequate nutrition and shelter. I focus my attention mostly on the connection between *decency and the rule of law*. I thus interpret decency as prescribing effective an appropriate and effective voice for all persons and peoples as participants in global cooperation. In this respect, I align decency with the criteria of domination and non-domination, familiar from classical and neo-republican theory. Here, domination consists in the effective denial of access to the rule of law to at least some social participants, rendering them unable to shape its future contests through contestations and dissent commanding uptake and reconsideration. Non-domination, by contrast, consist is the ability of the latter indeed to gain such access by commanding uptake and reconsideration. To be sure, Rawls himself does not make any explicit appeal to the republican standard of non-domination, although he does acknowledge that his liberal theory of justice is consistent with republicanism (2005).

That said, I contend civil disobedience is a good conceptual fit with the ideal of non-domination insofar as disobedients contest failures of the rule of law to guarantee an effective political voice for all participants in cooperation. Nevertheless, the normative significance of the appeal to decency as grounding civil disobedience in a global perspective is that it permits an *extension* of justifiable disobedience beyond the confines of the liberal-democratic state. The justification for civil disobedience is applicable to any context of politics in which the rule of law is disordered and merely piecewise just in the sense that it does not guarantee an effective political voice for some participants in cooperation. Indeed, the concept of the rule of law is broader than the liberal conception of social justice endorsed by Rawls as epitomizing the moral character of liberal peoples. In this light, he develops in *Law of Peoples* (2001) the hypothetical conception of a non-liberal or hierarchical society, whose ruling elite organize the people according to an alternative common good conception of justice. In such a non-liberal society, there are no equal civil and political rights of citizens. Nevertheless, its legitimacy fundamentally depends on the guarantee that citizens enjoy effective access to the rule of law through well-established consultation protocols in which they register their contestations and dissent.

The introduction of this hypothetical has enormous implications for the global perspective, not in the least of which is that disobedients may claim justification for their protests, even when they do not share commitments to liberal social justice. To this extent, I emphasize that, in all three of my cases, disobedients may be the citizens from both liberal and hierarchical societies, as well as both liberal and peoples. Indeed, I call both persons and peoples resorting to justifiable civil disobedience in a global perspective 'cosmopolitan citizens.' This is consistent with a moderate cosmopolitanism about justice (Scheffler 1999), aligning with the Law of Peoples. Acknowledges moral obligations beyond their own borders, cosmopolitan citizens recognize the normative priority of states and peoples, as the primary sites of responsibility taking for human rights and the implementation of ongoing human rights *reform* (Beitz 2011). As either intra- or inter-state civil disobedients, they address states and peoples as responsible subjects for enacting such reforms and creating a global system, ordered according to shared decency commitments.

1.5 The Limits of Liberalism and the Positive Contribution of Non-liberal Viewpoints

One of Rawls' key motivations in writing *Law of Peoples* is to recognize that not all peoples are liberal and that a project of global justice as liberal social justice writ large (Held 2004) would necessarily contradict the liberal principle of toleration. It would contradict this principle by failing to show toleration for non-liberal points of view. I am sympathetic to this concern and acknowledge that a lack of toleration for decent but non-liberal viewpoints would contradict this principle. Nevertheless, my project is not primarily about toleration for non-liberal points of view, broadly consistent with international decency and minimal human rights standards. Instead, I aim to show that decent non-liberal – as well as liberal – conceptions of justice underwrite global civil disobedience practices, challenging the piecewise just condition of an unfair global system. In other words, decent but non-liberal conceptions are not simply the passive objects of liberal toleration. On the contrary, they are potential equal contributors to the positive advancement of global justice. In this respect, liberalism has no monopoly on the justification of disobedient protests by diverse cosmopolitan citizens. It has no such monopoly for, at least, two interconnected reasons:

1. Not all failures of global justice are reducible to piecewise failures of liberal social justice
2. Fundamental reform of the global system, in light of such injustices, requires justificatory grounds that do not fundamentally depend on liberal premises

Indeed, as the following chapters show, the injustices suffered by undocumented migrants are not reducible to a denial of citizenship rights in a liberal democracy. Consequently, the human right to be a political participant, wherever you are, is freestanding of liberal premises, concerning the moral equality of persons as the citizens of such a state. The same applies to the unfairness of global economic inequities: the promotion of liberal citizenship rights badly misconstrues the appropriate resolution of such systematic global unfairness. Moreover, the broad concerns about publicity and the ends of government raised by executive prerogative and disobedient disclosure are not exclusively the concerns of liberal governments and liberal citizens.

After having discussed the above cases in the proceeding chapters, I return to the idea that liberalism has no monopoly on the justificatory grounds for civil disobedience in the concluding chapter of this book. Not only do I affirm that non-liberal viewpoints can make equal positive contributions to global justice through the participation of diverse cosmopolitan citizens in global disobedience practices, but also I offer an analytical redefinition of civil disobedience, in light of my three cases. This redefinition stresses the justificatory significance of decency in such global practices. Indeed, adhering to both liberal and non-liberal viewpoints, cosmopolitan citizen disobedients jointly contribute to an ongoing discourse of decency, grounding civilly disobedient challenges to piecewise failures of justice in the global system. The redefinition retains certain key features of the state-centered theory of disobedience, especially the idea that fair terms of cooperation requires a fair value of liberty in shaping the contents of law and rights. Nevertheless, it departs from the state-centered theory when it comes to the question of whom the international community owes such a value in global cooperation. It does so by extending this concern, under the rubric of international decency, to the undocumented and resource-poor peoples, along with any who could act through either secrecy or disclosure in defense of the ends of decent government.

1.6 Outline of Chapters

Chapter 2 develops some preliminary themes. After laying out the concepts of peoples and decency from *Law of Peoples*, I argue that decency is a moral consideration capable of defeating the duty to obey. I then develop a connection between decency and non-domination to which I return repeatedly in the subsequent chapters. The connection of decency to non-domination may seem surprising given its strong association with modern or neo-Roman republicanism. Nevertheless, I show that decency entails non-domination, in a very general sense, by legitimizing contestation and dissent from the (domestic and international) rule of law. Chapter 3 takes up the case of the undocumented. Here, I defend the idea that the undocumented are a special category of civil disobedients, under the circumstances of globalization, especially vulnerable to both interpersonal and systemic forms of domination and exploitation. Indeed, their vulnerability to ongoing domination is more urgent than that of refugees. Here, I argue that decency prescribes that the undocumented are entitled to at least minimal participatory political rights. Appealing to a particular case study of the undocumented in the United States, Chapter 4 builds on the preceding discussion by arguing for a human right to be a political participant wherever you are. This novel addition to the list of human rights recognized by the *Law of Peoples* is a global requirement of decency and indeed a reform of law and policy necessary to address the plight of undocumented persons. I argue for institutionally embedding the human right to be a political participant, wherever you are, in the basic institutional structures of all decency societies, liberal and non-liberal.

Chapter 5 turns to a global perspective on civil disobedience in the context of global economic inequities. It offers a third way between duties of assistance to the poor and global distributive justice. It does so by highlighting instead the normative equality assigned to *peoples* in the *Law of Peoples*. I argue that disobedience is justified by the unfair value of the liberty among rich and poor peoples, whereby the former to dominate the processes of international law making in their economic self-interest. I argue for a reinterpretation of the duty of assistance not as distributing resources to the global poor, but creating a reformed international order in which all peoples enjoy *a fair value of liberty* in shaping international law and policy. I show that this is indeed a prescription of decency. Chapter 6 then addresses the quite different issue of competing modes of extra-legality both of which may be justified by appeal to decency. As in the previous chapter on global economic inequities, I do not argue in favor of any new human right, like a human right to transparency. Instead, I argue for peoples to undertake a deep reconsideration of the entailments of decency, in light of the complexity of global politics. This ultimately becomes a concern with fairness and leniency in sentencing officials and disclosers with equally valid justifications for acting contrary to the law.

Finally, Chapter 7 ties together these discussions by focusing the goal of civil disobedience in a global perspective as the creation of global solidarity with those rendered vulnerable to domination and exploitation in the complex processes of globalization. The chapter also offers an analytical redefinition of civil disobedience in light of my various case studies.

References

Allen, Michael. 2011a. Civil Disobdience, Transnational. In *Encyclopedia of Global Justice*, ed. Deen Chatterjee, vol. 1, 135–137. Dordrecht: Springer.
———. 2011b. Civil Disobedience, International. In *Encyclopedia of Global Justice*, ed. Deen Chatterjee, vol. 1, 133–135. Dordrecht: Springer.
Arendt, Hannah. 2000. What Is Freedom? In *The Portable Hannah Arendt*, ed. Peter Baehr, 438–461. London: Penguin Books.
Beitz, Charles. 2011. *The Idea of Human Rights*. Oxford: Oxford University Press.
———. 2008. Justice and International Relations. In *Global Justice Seminal Essays*, ed. Thomas Pogge and Darrel Moellendorf. St. Paul: Paragon House.
Benthouami, Hourya. 2007. Civil Disobedience from Thoreau to Transnational Mobilizations: The Global Challenge. *Essays in Philosophy* 8(2): Article 3.
Buchanan, Allen. 2007. *Legitimacy, Justice, and Self-Determination*. Oxford: Oxford University Press.
Caney, Simon. 2006. *Justice Beyond Borders: A Global Political Theory*. Oxford: Oxford University Press.
Carens, Joseph. 1987. Aliens and Citizens: The Case for Open Borders. *Review of Politics* 49(2): 251–273.
Corlett, Angelo. 2003. *Terrorism: A Philosophical Analysis*. Dordrecht: Springer.
Gandhi, Mohandas. 1932. *Yervada Mandir*. Trans. V.G. Desai. Ahmedabad: Navjivan.
Goodin, Robert. 2005. Towards and International Rule of Law: Distinguishing International Law-Breakers from Would-be Law-Makers. *Journal of Ethics* 9(1-2): 225–246.
Griffin, James. 2008. *On Human Rights*. Oxford: Oxford University Press.
Held, David. 2004. *Global Covenant: The Social Democratic Alternative to the Washington Consensus*. Cambridge: Polity.
Kokaz, Nancy. 2005. Theorizing International Fairness. *Metaphilosophy* 36: 68–92.
Miller, David. 2012. *National Responsibility and Global Justice*. Oxford: Oxford University Press.
Nagel, Thomas. 2005. The Problem of Global Justice. *Philosophy and Public Affairs* 33(2): 113–147.
Ogunye, Temi. 2015. Global Justice and Transnational Civil Disobedience. *Ethics and Global Politics* 8(1). doi:10.3402/egp.v8.27217.
Rawls, John. 2005. *Political Liberalism*. New York: Columbia University Press.
———. 2001. *The Law of Peoples*. Cambridge, MA: Harvard University Press.
———. 1971. *A Theory of Justice*. Cambridge, MA: Harvard University Press.
Risse, Mathias. 2015. *On Global Justice*. Princeton: Princeton University Press.
Sabl, Andrew. 2003. Looking Forward to Justice: Rawlsian Civil Disobedience and its Non-Rawlsian Lessons. *Journal of Political Philosophy* 9(3): 307–330.
Scheffler, Samuel. 1999. Conceptions of Cosmopolitanism. *Utilitas* 11: 255–276.
Thoreau, Henry David. 1993. *Civil Disobedience*. Dover Publications.
Von Essen, Erica. 2017. Environmental Disobedience and the Dialogic Dimension of Dissent. *Democratization*. doi:10.1080/13510347.2016.1185416.
Welchman, Jennifer. 2001. Is Ecosabotage Civil Disobedience? *Philosophy and Geography* 4(1): 97–107.

Chapter 2
Decency, the Right to Disobey, and Non-domination

Abstract This chapter builds upon the idea sketched in the introduction of civil disobedience as a global practice, grounded in commitments to international decency standards. It first lays out the idea of decency as an international standard of accountability for peoples who are reasonable as well as rational. As an international standard, decency does not apply only to the familiar case of domestic disobedience in liberal-democratic states. Neither does it insist upon liberal-democratic premises as paradigmatic of global justice. Instead, it embraces alternative traditional-hierarchical perspectives of justice. The chapter, then, develops this idea as the basis for justifiable disobedient action in the global arena, placing both liberal-democratic and traditional-hierarchical peoples under binding obligations of uptake and reconsideration. This may entail uptake and reconsideration for domestic law and policy binding for either category of people, or uptake and reconsideration for international law and policy binding for all reasonable peoples. The chapter further links the idea of decency to a broad interpretation of non-domination as effective access to legal redress, domestically and internationally, through the protection of dissent and contestation.

2.1 Introduction

Civil disobedience has always presupposed the idea of states and peoples. As a mode of public address, civil disobedience engages a citizen-body, a people, who is the party ultimately responsible for ensuring that relations of justice internally and externally. That is, the people are responsible for ensuring the justice of relations within territorial borders not only between co-nationals but also between co-nationals and diverse kinds of non-nationals living within these borders. It is also responsible for ensuring that relations of justice obtain between itself and other national peoples. This conception of peoples aligns with the familiar idea of the normative priority of states for international or global justice (Risse 2015). According to this

M. Allen, *Civil Disobedience in Global Perspective*,
Studies in Global Justice 16, DOI 10.1007/978-94-024-1164-5_2

idea, states have normative priority for ensuring relations of justice, internally and externally, insofar as they remain the primary sites of accountability in the global order. In this global order, states delegate authority to many kinds of supra-states agencies – from, say, the United Nations or the World Bank – as the result of treaty-based agreements. Moreover, the enforcement of international agreements between states ultimately falls to states themselves, as ultimately possessing the requisite powers of enforcements (Beitz 2011; Miller 2012; Nagel 2005). Such normative priority of states, however, is derivative of the peoples they represent. Indeed, peoples authorize states as their agents to carry out their collective will according to their moral character.

The importance of these observations is that peoples to whom states are accountable are the most appropriate subject of disobedient public address. This follows not only in the case of internal disobedience between co-nationals of the same state, but also various sorts of intra-state disobedience campaigns between non-national and co-national populations within state borders, as well as in the case of inter-state disobedience campaigns between different peoples across the multiple borders constituting the global order. Disobedient public address to peoples, however, assumes that different peoples share fundamental commitments to justice. Even if they do not share the same standards of internal, domestic justice obtaining between co-national citizens, different peoples must share fundamental commitments to international justice as a basis for globally consequential disobedient public address. Indeed, such shared international commitments are indispensable to successful public address, especially in cases in which peoples may differ in their conceptions of internal, domestic justice. After all, the addressees can hardly see themselves as bound to uptake and reconsideration when they reject the principles of justice to which disobedients appeal. In short, diverse relationships of disobedience, uptake, and reconsideration in the global arena of politics need shared principles of justice.

The *Law of Peoples* is helpful for my project of providing an account of such global disobedience relations to the extent it defines peoples in terms of their moral character and commitments to reasonableness and reciprocity in international relations. Here, decency captures the idea of reasonableness between peoples with different commitments to internal, domestic justice. More than a set of shared commitments to minimal standards of human rights, decency is the basis for a global discourse on the entailments of justice beyond the relations of co-nationals in the self-enclosed state. As I shall show in the subsequent chapters, such a discourse takes a number of different directions, which expand upon the present minimal list of human rights in Law of Peoples. My concern in this chapter, however, is primarily to show that the international standard of decency between peoples is capable of underwriting diverse global practices of civil disobedience, as promised in the introduction to this monograph. This requires me to show that decency can indeed underwrite a moral right to disobey binding different peoples to uptake and reconsideration in various intra- and inter-state contexts of injustice. In this respect, I assume that the global system is in a condition of only nearly (Rawls 1971) or piecewise (Sabl 2003) justice (also see Ogunye 2015). From the perspective of decency, different peoples ought to acknowledge the justifiability of civil disobedience as defeating the duty to obey and binding them to consider fundamental amendments to the Law of Peoples.

In this latter respect, civil disobedience is always about breaking the law in order to remake the law (Buchanan 2007). It is a standpoint of respect for the rule of law and its relationship to protecting the moral equality of persons. Ultimately, the rule of law protects persons by affording them a secure status guaranteeing immunity from different forms of persecution, oppression, and domination. Neo-republican idea of freedom as non-domination captures this concern with enjoying the protection of the rule of law (Pettit 1997). In its broadest sense, the guarantee of non-domination is the legal right of dissent from the present legal order without fear of reprisal or retaliation. I offer an interpretation of decency between peoples in light of this broad sense of non-domination. A crucial feature of the Law of Peoples is the commitment of all decent and reasonable peoples to guaranteeing effective access to the basic elements of the rule of law, which necessarily entails extending protected rights of dissent and contestation to those subject to laws (Rawls 2001; Beitz 2011). Here, the subjects of law could be the citizens of either liberal-democratic or traditional-hierarchical societies, they could be non-nationals living within the borders of either type of society, or they could be peoples bound under the treaty obligations of international law. In all of these cases, the legitimacy of law depends on the subjects of law enjoying secure and effective rights of dissent and contestation. Indeed, the arguments of the subsequent chapters aim to show that many of the diverse subjects of law in the global system do not presently enjoy security with respect to effective access to the rule of law; hence, the global system remains only piecewise. Consequently, disobedience appealing to the global criterion of decency aims at a global order of non-domination among peoples.

This, however, need not entail some total reconfiguration the Law of Peoples in terms of a global republican constitution, reminiscent of Kant or more recent accounts of republicanism and global justice. Instead, it remains consistent with the emphasis of Law of Peoples on alternative conceptions of justice binding of different peoples: that is, peoples ordered in different ways, but entering into a discourse on emerging global relations of justice by virtue of their shared commitments to decency. I arrange his chapter in four sections. The first considers the ideas of peoples and decency in Law of Peoples, while the second develops an account of decency as underwriting global practices of civil disobedience. The third section then discusses the relationship between decency and the broad interpretation of non-domination. Finally, the fourth justifies my use of Rawls' controversial concept of the traditional-hierarchical society, in light of a common objection to it as a hypothetical construction.

2.2 Peoples and Decency

Rawls defines peoples as relevantly different from states, but also as related to states. Indeed, states are amoral rational-prudential actors exercising the traditional right and powers of sovereignty. These include the external right of autonomy to go to war, as an exercise of politics by other means (Clausewitz 2013), and the internal right of autonomy to do as they will with their own peoples within their own borders. By contrast, Rawls conceives of peoples as possessing a moral character. Indeed, peoples express their moral character through authorizing the government of their state. Authorization thus establishes a relation of peoples to state as a relationship to political authority (Avila 2005). In the case of a liberal-democratic state, government is authorization rationally through a process of majoritarian voting. In the case of non-democratic states, peoples may authorize their governments differently through hierarchical, or stratified, procedures of consultation (Rawls 2001). Authorized by either electoral or consultation process, government subsequently enacts law and policy in the people's name. Nevertheless, democratic and hierarchical peoples are not merely *rational* actors. Their collective acts of authorizing a government to act in their name are appropriately constrained by their sense of what is *reasonable*.

In terms of internal sovereignty, the reasonableness of a constitutional liberal-democratic people is expressed by the willingness of citizens to offer fair terms of cooperation to one another as co-authors of the state's domestic laws and policies, provided their compatriots reciprocally honor these terms (Rawls 2005). Here, fair terms of cooperation between liberal-democratic citizens require equal political participation rights in elections and voting. Hierarchical peoples express reasonableness in a different way, based on differential rights of group memberships, as opposed to individual rights. Indeed, the officials of such societies represent citizens non-electorally through hierarchical procedures of consultation based on such memberships and group rights (Rawls 2001). Nonetheless, their behavior internationally may still mirror that of liberal-democratic peoples. In international rather domestic politics, reasonableness entails the people's willingness to offer fair terms of cooperation with others peoples, and to honor these terms when assured that other peoples will do the same (Rawls 2001). To this extent, both liberal-democratic and hierarchical peoples satisfy an appropriate standard of reasonableness *applicable to international relations*, even if they do not share the *same standards of reasonableness for individual persons* applicable in liberal-democracies.

In addition to the contrast between peoples and states, Rawls contrasts *peoples* with *individual persons*. Indeed, reciprocally abiding by terms of international cooperation, liberal-democratic and hierarchical peoples are *free and equal* in their relations to one another qua peoples. That is, they are free and equal in the exchange of terms of cooperation as collective moral agents each possessing their own distinctive character. In this respect, their freedom and equality is similar to that of individual persons as citizens of the liberal-democratic state. It is similar in that different peoples may offer and accept terms of cooperation based upon their powers of moral agency. Nevertheless, it is also different in that the exchange of terms by such different peoples does not presuppose the freedom and equality of individual persons in reciprocally offering terms of cooperation. This priority on the moral equality and reasonableness of individual persons remains a distinctive concern of liberal-democratic peoples, and it is *not* the foundation of international relations and global justice from the standpoint of the *Law of Peoples*.

Here, it is important to stress that that the *Law of Peoples* does not repudiate the idea of the moral equality of all individual persons. Not, at any rate, when this is understood in the broad sense of equal consideration with respect to realizing a special class of *urgent* human rights to liberty (although not equal liberty of conscience and political participation for all individuals), along with life and limb, property, and the satisfaction of basic economic needs (Rawls 2001). In this respect, the difference between liberal-democratic and hierarchical peoples, regarding the moral equality of persons, lies in how they see the realization of such urgent human rights as related or not related to equal citizenship rights. In his earlier *A Theory of Justice* (1971), Rawls argued that equal rights citizenship are instrumental to realizing the other urgent rights of individual persons. To this extent, he insisted the justification for civil disobedience ought to appeal *only* to violations of equal liberty and fair equality of opportunity rights, assuming the free exercise of such equal citizenship rights is sufficient to guarantee all other urgent rights, such as rights to economic security.

By contrast, hierarchical peoples do not attribute the same instrumentality to liberal citizenship rights. Instead, they see their own stratified protocols of representation and consultation as instrumental to realizing urgent rights of humanity. Equal citizenship rights, manifest through voting and universal suffrage, is not an urgent human right at all, but rather a feature of how liberal-democratic peoples express their moral character and organize their societies differently. Neither does Rawls see voting and universal suffrage as an urgent human right. Liberalism and democracy can be detached from global justice. This opens up the possibility of justifications for civil disobedience in terms of the broader category of decency to which I shall turn in a moment. Suffice it to say for now that equal consideration for the urgent rights of individual persons do not necessarily depend on the guarantees of equal liberty or fair equality of opportunity Rawls insisted upon in *Theory*. This, of course, does not require that traditional-hierarchical peoples to deny that liberal-democratic citizenship rights can be instrumental to the satisfaction of urgent human rights. However, they would deny they are necessary as the only instruments to such an end. This is a point on which Rawls, on pain of consistency, would be bound to agree. At most, he could appeal to arguments to the effect that democracy is a more efficient means to the end of human rights (for example, Sen 2000), and not that it is the only means.

Rawls works out the idea of decency with respect to upholding urgent human rights standards in direct relation to his idea of a hierarchical people. In this respect, he offers two criteria for the decency of such peoples. First, they do not have aggressive aims and respect the sovereignty of other peoples. Nevertheless, this alone does not distinguish hierarchical from liberal-democratic peoples. Both are free and equal qua peoples to the extent they meet the criterion of non-aggression and respect for sovereignty. The second criterion for decency, however, does, entail some substantial differences from liberal-democratic peoples. Decent hierarchical peoples must (a) have a system of law ordered by a common good conception of justice, which must (b) impose bona fide moral duties and obligations on all persons within the peoples' territory. Moreover, (c) judges and other officials, administering the legal system, must act on a sincere belief in this conception. To this extent, the second decency criterion, worked out in relation to such societies, specifies a legal system, *but without* the civil and political egalitarianism characteristic of liberal-democratic societies.

Nevertheless, this emphasis on the rule of law in a hierarchical society defines another urgent human right: that is, an urgent right of effective access to the basic elements of the rule of law. The satisfaction of the other urgent human rights to liberty (if not equal liberty of conscience and political participation), life, limb, and the satisfaction of basic economic needs entail that there should always be a guarantee of such access to the rule of law. In other words, effective access to the rule of law is a requirement of decency, even though rule of law need not be that specific to a liberal-democratic people. Both types of peoples thus regard their characteristic institutional arrangements – organized under the domestic rule of law – as instrumental to realizing entirely generalizable interests of all persons. To this extent, there is a considerable overlap between hierarchical and liberal democratic societies concerning such generalizable interests. Indeed, while worked out in relation to the former type of society, the second criterion of decency highlights effective access to the rule of law and its connection to promoting generalizable interests of all humanity.

That said, however, I claimed in the introduction to this chapter that decency establishes relations and duties of justice underwriting global practices of civil disobedience. With this in mind, I turn now to an account of decency as the basis of moral considerability for the moral right to disobey in a merely piecewise just global system.

2.3 Decency as the Basis of Moral Considerability for the Right to Disobey

I have argued, then, that decency ought to be understood less in terms of any specific set of institutional arrangements and more in terms of what ends or goals different kinds of arrangements under the rule of law. Consequently, any set of institutional arrangements – liberal-democratic or otherwise – will count as decent if they facilitate securing the urgent rights of humanity. Nevertheless, is decency a moral consideration capable of defeating the duty to obey? Is it, in other words, a viable basis for justifiable practices of intra- and inter-state civil disobedience, such as those I sketched in the introduction to this monograph? Indeed, the first of these concerned intra-state disobedience practices between co-nationals within territorial borders. Here, such practices take on a global perspective to the extent that all decent peoples, and not just liberal-democratic peoples, acknowledge the legitimacy of disobedient dissent from the domestic rule of law. This, however, obviously demands an argument for the justifiability of such dissent that hierarchical peoples could acknowledge, based upon the goals of their distinctive institutional arrangements and commitments to the rule of law.

In this respect, I stress that the duty to obey obtains only in societies that have a legitimate claim to political authority (see, for instance, Lefkowitz

2007). Nearly or piecewise just societies have such a claim to legitimacy insofar as they realize justice for most of the co-national people most of the time within national borders. Nevertheless, the duty to obey may be defeated in those instances in which some of the people experience clear and substantial injustices (Rawls 1971; Sabl 2003). Of course, in his *Theory* (1971), Rawls himself equates these injustices with violations of the principles of equal liberty and fair equality of opportunity (p. 372), thereby undermining the goals of justice entertained exclusively by liberal-democratic peoples. What, though, of traditional-hierarchical peoples who do not subscribe to the same principles? Can they also acknowledge circumstances in which the duty to obey is defeated, but without reference to equal liberty and fair equality of opportunity? My answer is yes insofar as decency substitutes for these principles as defeating considerations for the duty to obey.

After all, violations of urgent human rights to liberty (if not liberty of conscience or political participation), life, limb, property, and basic economic security necessarily undermine the goals of justice for hierarchical peoples they are to achieve through their institutional arrangements. Likewise, the lack of any effective access to legal redress through those consultation hierarchies laid out in these arrangements necessarily undermines such goals. Consequently, the citizens of hierarchical societies should acknowledge clear and substantial violations of urgency and decency as considerations potentially defeating the duty to obey. Not to acknowledge this possibility of justifiable disobedience would be to contradict the idea of a people defined by its moral character and commitment to principles. It would collapse the Rawlsian distinction between people and state, where the role of the former is to authorize the latter, as political authority, based on commitments to principles of justice. Indeed, failure to acknowledge the legitimacy of civil disobedience, grounded in urgency and decency as opposed to equal liberty and fair equality of opportunity, would signify a failure of the moral character of a hierarchical people.

However, a possible objection is that, even if they provide an in-principle justification for civil disobedience in a hierarchical society, urgency and decency do not provide a basis of general public address. The idea of civil disobedience presupposes that disobedients should address the people as a whole. Indeed, this is required for the people to express its collective moral character through uptake and reconsideration of the piecewise nature of justice in the institutional arrangements of society. It further presupposes that the public should possess equal political participation rights as the basis for giving expression to its considered moral judgements regarding these arrangements. In other words, civilly disobedient public address entails the institutional arrangements specific to a liberal-democratic society. The people as a whole must be capable of entering into a robust process of democratic public deliberation, as free and equal political participants. At any rate, the society must be sufficiently piecewise just in its commitments to liberal-democratic arrangements for most of the people to enter into such democratic public deliberative processes. If correct, this objection would not rule out civil disobedience within a hierarchical society on in-principle grounds. After all, civil disobedients could still defend their action before the moral conscience of the people. Nevertheless, the society lacks the kinds of institutional arrangements necessary for a *practice* of civil disobedience to emerge insofar as that entails democratic public deliberation.

This objection, however, is hardly compelling. Here, it is helpful to consider an important distinction offered by David Lefkowitz (2007) between public deliberation and public communication. On the one hand, public deliberation entails a strong tie to the idea of democratic participation. Such participation may be inclusive of democratic majoritarianism and the casting of votes by free and equal citizens. Nevertheless, it also entails more than majoritarianism and voting. Indeed, rather than simply casting votes and then leaving the task of deliberation to their elected representatives, citizens themselves should be participants in the process of deliberating the contents of law and policy (for instance, Smith 2013 and Markovits 2005). On the other hand, public communication entails a much weaker tie o democratic participation by free and equal citizens. It entails only that members of the public should be able to communicate their grievances and concerns to appropriate officials of the state. It does not also entail that citizens should be participants in the deliberating and shaping the contents of law and policy. To this extent, deliberation over these contents is not 'public' as much as it is 'official' deliberation.

Based on Lefkowitz's distinction between public deliberation and public communication, a justifiable practice of civil disobedience emerges in cases in which there is a *deficit* of deliberation, either public or official. That is, a practice emerges when disobedients address *either* the democratic public of free and equal citizens *or* the officials of the state as those parties responsible for deliberating and reconsidering law and policy in light of the piecewise nature of justice in the society. Here, deliberation deficits are failures to reconsider law and policy when there are good reasons for believing that the present arrangements of society only incompletely realize those demands of justice definitive of the collective moral character of the people. For instance, deficits of deliberation may result from the imposition of time-limits on the process of reaching public decisions, or from the practical necessity of accepting difficult compromises in cases of deep controversy, leaving fundamental grievances unresolved (Markovits 2005). Alternatively, they may arise as the result of asymmetries of social power, as when rich and powerful individuals, families, or corporations use their superior prestige and material resources to exert undue influence in shaping the processes of public or official deliberation to their advantage (Smith 2013).

Under these circumstances, disobedients may claim justification for their actions as aiming to restart stalled or blocked deliberation processes among *either* public *or* officials presently hostage to compromise or power. To this extent, they may properly bind either addressee of disobedience to a practice of uptake and reconsideration. Nonetheless, the importance of Lefkowitz's distinction lies in the possibility of its establishing a practice of disobedience, uptake, and reconsideration through public communication alone. In other words, a practice appealing only to official and not public deliberation of clear and substantial injustices in the piecewise just order. Such a possibility encompasses traditional-hierarchical society in which there is no democratic public of free and equal citizens. As noted in the previous section, hierarchically ordered peoples already engage in public communication with officials, registering their grievances to officials through various consultation protocols (Rawls 2001). Granting they are no less vulnerable to deliberation deficits in which they become hostage to compromises and asymmetric social powers than their counterparts in liberal-democracies, the officials of traditional-hierarchical societies are therefore equally bound to give uptake for public communication that is civilly disobedient. To this extent, civil disobedience is not only defensible before the moral conscience of hierarchically ordered peoples, but also the institutional arrangements of their societies satisfy the prerequisites for binding disobedients and officials in a practice of uptake and reconsideration.

Hence, contrary to the objection considered above, democracy is not an exclusive institutional prerequisite for civil disobedience.[1] Indeed, the disobedience practice of a traditional-hierarchical society is made possible (1) by its people's commitment to urgency and decency rather than equal liberty and fair equality of opportunity and (2) by a hierarchical arrangement of basic institutions designed to realize the former, not the latter, principles of justice. Indeed, the crucial feature of this argument is that considerations of urgency and decency defeat the duty to obey, thus rendering obedience

[1] To be sure, Lefkowitz himself insists that public communication should remain attached to democratic majoritarianism and voting. In this respect, he appeals to the utility of periodic election cycles for replacing unresponsive representatives. Here, universal suffrage and majoritarian voting may well possess such utility, even without public deliberation: that is certainly not in contention. Nevertheless, the point remains that a disobedience practice – absent any of the core institutional features of democracy – is a fully intelligible prospect.

unreasonable. Appealing to T. M. Scanlon's (2000) method of reasonable rejection, Lefkowitz claims: "a moral agent's natural duties to refrain from treating others in various ways that they could reasonably reject correlate with the rights of others not to be treated in those ways" (2007, p. 206). Such rights of others that could not reasonably be rejected include – while not being limited to – "basic or human rights" (Ibid); that is, the special class of urgent human rights laid out in *Law of Peoples* (2001). Moreover, correlative "to these rights are duties on all other moral agents to see to it that they are not violated" (Lefkowitz 2007, p. 207).

Building on Lefkowitz's Scanlonian insight, disobedient public communication is one way in which those moral agents, who are also the citizens of traditional-hierarchical societies, *can see to it* that officials uphold urgent human rights no decent people could reasonably reject. But, if it is individually reasonable for citizens to reject the duty to obey by appeal to urgent human rights, then by parity of reasoning the officials whom they address through civil disobedience cannot reasonably reject their appeals for reconsideration, based on the same criteria. Here, the principle of reasonable rejection applies not to the reasonableness of individuals but rather peoples. After all, officials are agents of the people representing its collective moral character. To this extent, they cannot reasonably reject uptake and reconsideration, when urgent human rights are at stake. Nonetheless, they could reasonably reject disobedient public communication claiming violations of equal liberty and fair equality of opportunity, as principles of justice defining the quite different moral character of liberal-democratic peoples.

So far, I have argued that an intra-state practice of disobedience is possible among hierarchically ordered co-nationals, in addition to the free and equal citizens of democracies. Nevertheless, this still leaves open the questions of intra-state disobedience practices between non-nationals and co-national peoples as well as inter-state practices between different peoples. These, however, are the cases I explore in depth in the subsequent chapters of this monograph. As such, I do not provide any detailed discussion of them here. Suffice it to say, for now, that all cases appeal to the principle of reasonable rejection as applied to peoples. Indeed, I argue that individuals who are non-nationals may reasonably reject the duty to obey the laws of co-national peoples by appeal to urgent human rights. Indeed, no peoples – liberal-democratic or hierarchical – can reasonably reject such disobedient public communication. Moreover, different peoples engaged in inter-state disobedient public communication with other peoples regarding urgent human rights violations in international, as opposed to domestic, law bind one another to uptake and reconsideration. That is, peoples bind peoples, again, according to the reasonable rejection principle.

I next offer some remarks on what I take to be the key feature of the decency criteria of the Law of Peoples: that all peoples owe all persons, as well as all other peoples, access to the rule of law and the guarantee of effective legal redress for their grievances concerning urgent human rights claims. Indeed, in the proceeding chapters, I describe the failure of peoples to create institutional conditions, domestically and internationally, providing such a guarantee as the conditions of domination. As I employ this term, domination is either the condition in which moral agents – individual or collective – have no recognized status as protected under the rule of law, or only an insecure status, leaving them vulnerable to other injustices of harassment and persecution.

2.4 Decency, the Rule of Law, and Non-domination

Nevertheless, my appeal to domination in relation to the decency criteria from *Law of Peoples* requires some preliminary justification. Rawls himself does not use the language of domination. Moreover, the ideas of domination and non-domination are often reflexively associated with a modern neo-republican conception of law, government, and freedom (for example, Pettit 1997; Maynor 2003). Indeed, neo-republicanism is committed to the idea of the moral equality of persons as citizens. To this extent, its basic commitments would appear to be no different from liberal-democracies, as discussed by Rawls (see his 1994 for a discussion of classical republicanism in relation to liberal-democracy, p. 205). Nevertheless, such egalitarianism appears to contradict the differential distribution of rights and duties among citizen of traditional-hierarchical societies, as conceived by Rawls (2001). Any notion of a clash between non-domination and the decency criterion of *Law of Peoples*, however, simply confuses domination with the very different concept of tyranny.

Indeed, tyranny and not domination is the proper contrast with the rule of law. More often than not, tyranny is linked to the absolutist idea that the 'will of the prince is law.' John Locke (1998) captures this version of tyranny in his memorable phrase that 'where law ends, tyranny begins. In other words, tyranny is the ending or absence of any 'rule of law and not men.' By contrast, domination is a condition that necessarily exists under the rule of law: it is an injustice within legal or judicial parameters (Skinner 2013; Pettit 1997; Maynor 2003). This intrinsic tie between domination and law should be apparent from the contrast in classical Roman republicanism between freeman and slave. The freeman is free to the extent he is a recognized person under law, with guaranteed rights and immunities against servitude. These rights and immunities mean that, as a legal person, he enjoys the condition of freedom from domination.

Nevertheless, this legal status also permits the freeman, who is also a slaveholder, to act arbitrarily towards his slave. Nevertheless, the freeman's cruel and arbitrary treatment of the slave is not a species of tyranny that begins where law ends. After all, the law *protects* the freeman in his ability to dispose of his property – that is, his human chattel – *as he sees fit* and as the law permits. The freeman is thus not a tyrant, but rather a dominator protected in his capacity to *subordinate another human being by the law* (for a recent discussion of domination as grounded in judicial authority, see Blunt 2015). Positioning domination in terms of classical Roman republicanism is important to the present study for a number of reasons.

One is that, unlike tyranny, domination aligns with the Rawlsian idea of piecewise justice in which the rule of law and its protections and benefits are regularly accessible to some but not others. Not only is this the particular circumstance of justice in which the Rawlsian conception of civil disobedience applies. As I have shown, however, it is also a circumstance potentially arising in all societies claiming to be decent, including traditional-hierarchical societies. Indeed, no society claiming to be decent can be a tyranny, in the sense that regular and reliable access to the rule of law is inaccessible to everyone. Nevertheless, decent societies may be only piecewise just. As such, they may manifest problems of domination denying access to the rule of law as an urgent human right to some persons, leaving them without legal redress, in some appropriate manner.

Another, and I believe obvious point, is that the classical Roman republic was clearly not a liberal-democracy based on equal liberty and fair equality of opportunity. Indeed, as emphasized above, free Roman citizens enjoyed protection of their 'right' to own slaves under law. If nothing else, this obvious point establishes that *non-domination* – as the guarantee of regular and reliable access to the rule of law – has no historical or intrinsic tie to liberalism or democracy, although it may be adapted to both (Pettit 1997; Maynor 2003). Nevertheless, and perhaps more importantly, Hegel in his *Philosophy of Right* (1998) aligns an apparently illiberal and non-democratic stratified order of differentially represented estates with non-domination (for instance, Buchwalter 2001; Allen 2006). To this extent, there are indeed precedents for its adaptation to hierarchical social orders.

Consistent with this conceptual independence of egalitarian democracy and adaptation to hierarchical order, however, non-domination also aligns with the concept of public communication I previously discussed. Indeed, the ultimate guarantee of freedom from domination is the protected right of ongoing dissent and contestation (Pettit 1997). Nevertheless, this does not depend on democratic public deliberation over law and policy-making. It depends instead on the commitment of officials and policy-makers to tracking generalizable or common interests and providing uptake for dissenting public communication should the former fail to deliver on their promises to promote such interests (Ibid). This is not to deny a possible alignment of non-domination with egalitarian democracy and public deliberation. It is to say, however, to say that public communication is sufficient for non-domination in a hierarchical order.

In light of these considerations, connecting non-domination to decency and urgent human rights, under the Law of Peoples, should not seem so surprising, after all. Indeed, the denial of access to the rule of law and its protections should no more be tolerated by traditional- hierarchical peoples than by liberal-democratic peoples.[2]

2.5 A Note on Democracy, Egalitarianism, and Hierarchy

Finally, I offer a brief note on democracy, egalitarianism, and hierarchy by way of justification for my use of Rawls' concept of the hierarchical society. Here, empirically minded critics might object that the concept has no sociological or political-scientific grounding in the description of any actually existing society. I have some sympathy for this kind of criticism. Nevertheless, I believe it is important to keep in mind Rawls' actual purpose in *Law of Peoples*. Rawls uses this concept as a hypothetical construction intended to provide an example of an alternative legitimation structure to constitutional liberal-democracies (2001). His purpose is not to lay out a description of any actual society, but rather to lay out legitimacy conditions, based on urgent human rights, *independently* of liberal-democratic ideals. Indeed, this is the value of his contribution to the global justice debate, as I see it. His motivation in doing this was to avoid the assumption that *only* such ideals can legitimately ground global justice and human rights.

[2] Clearly, a hierarchical society, such as the hypothetical Islamic society of Kazanistan imagined by Rawls (2001), might not consider itself a 'republic,' if it grounds its common good conception of justice in a comprehensive religious doctrine (2005). Nevertheless, even here some caution is in order. Iran, for instance, might be better described as a piecewise just society, based on the rule of law, than an outright tyranny. Moreover, it explicitly self-identifies as an Islamic Republic. At the very least, it is a theocratic-republican hybrid. Nevertheless, the crucial point here is its decency entails non-domination, according to the criterion of urgent human rights.

In this respect, he might be seen as motivated by a concern with avoiding liberal imperialism (for example, Mann 2005) and, more particularly, the kind self-contradiction concerning the liberal principle of toleration, which as a matter of consistency should extend to the toleration of non-liberal, non-democratic points of view (2001). Nevertheless, my own interest in the legitimacy of hierarchical orders, eschewing the equal rights and liberties of citizens, is somewhat different from Rawls. Indeed, as noted in the introductory chapter, my interest is not in avoiding liberal imperialism or self-contradiction concerning toleration. Instead, it is in thinking through the legitimacy conditions for relations of disobedience, uptake, and reconsideration not defined by equality among co-national citizens. In the case of undocumented disobedients, the disobedience relation is one of inequality and hierarchy between co-nationals and non-nationals. It is unequal and hierarchical to the extent the former exercise exclusive sovereign rights and powers over the latter.

Moreover, in the case of peoples as disobedients, the relation is one of inequality and hierarchy between different peoples. Here, disobedient peoples challenge the inequality of peoples in a global economic system hierarchically ordered in the interest of the richest and most powerful nation states. As for the case of disobedient disclosers, especially complex relations of disobedience emerge in response to inequality and hierarchy that necessarily result from secretive decision-making by state officials. Indeed, even in liberal-democracies, government secrecy assumes a hierarchy of officials suspending publicity and transparency guarantees for 'free and equal' citizens. The relevance of the concepts of inequality and hierarchy from *Law of Peoples* become apparent in these various cases of civil disobedience in a global perspective. In this global context, different kinds of disobedience must be justified not only absent the egalitarian premises of liberal-democracy. They also must be justified across personal inequalities based on different national identifications, and despite relations of hierarchy based on power or officials of states purporting to act for the common or public good.

Here, Rawls' emphasis in *Law of Peoples* on thinking through the conditions of justice amid inequality and hierarchy functions as a heuristic for civil disobedience in global perspective. It requires the theorist to confront inequality and hierarchy in the present global order of states and peoples. Indeed, to this extent, I extrapolate the discussion of inequality and hierarchy from the particular case of traditional-hierarchical peoples in *Law of Peoples* to the cases I discuss in the subsequent chapters. In each case, I explore the justifiability of disobedience under a quite different condition of global inequality and hierarchy.

2.6 Conclusion

In this chapter, I have laid the foundation for my subsequent discussions of civil disobedience in a global perspective by discussing the moral character of peoples in terms of their commitments to urgent human rights. I have argued that such rights are defeating considerations for the duty to obey demanding uptake from all decent peoples. The claims of disobedients – co-nationals, non-nationals or other peoples – create obligations of official deliberation, public deliberation, or both, depending on contextual differences in the circumstances and relations of justice entailed by disobedience. I have further argued that decent but piecewise just peoples who *un*reasonably reject urgent human rights claims are not tyrants but dominators. They are dominators to the extent they deny access to basic elements of the rule of law and its protections to, at least, some persons over whom they claim territorial jurisdictional authority. This broad conception of domination applies equally to liberal and hierarchical peoples.

In the next chapter, I turn to the first of my three cases of civil disobedience in a global perspective: undocumented disobedients as indeed especially vulnerable to domination and persecution.

References

Allen, Michael. 2006. Hegel Between Non-Domination and Expressive Freedom: Capabilities, Perspectives, Democracy. *Philosophy and Social Criticism* 32(4): 493–512.

Avila, Mitchell. 2005. Defending a Law of Peoples: Political Liberalism and Decent Peoples. *Journal of Ethics* 11(1): 87–124.

Beitz, Charles. 2011. *The Idea of Human Rights*. Oxford: Oxford University Press.

Blunt, Gwilym. 2015. On the Source, Sites, and Modes of Domination. *Journal of Political Power* 8(1): 5–20.

Buchanan, Allen. 2007. *Justice, Legitimacy and Self-Determination*. Oxford: Oxford University Press.

Buchwalter, Andrew. 2001. Law, Culture, and Constitutionalism: Remarks on Hegel and Habermas. In *Beyond Liberalism and Communitarianism*, ed. Robert R. Williams. New York: State University of New York Press.

Clausewitz, Carl von. 2013. *On War*. Clausewitz Press.

Hegel, G.W.F. 1998. *Elements of the Philosophy of Right*. Allen W. Wood ed. Cambridge: Cambridge University Press.

Lefkowitz, David. 2007. On a Moral Right to Civil Disobedience. *Ethics* 117(2): 202–233.

Locke, John. 1998. In *Two Treatises of Government*, ed. Peter Laslett. Cambridge: Cambridge University Press.

Mann, Michael. 2005. *Incoherent Empire*. London: Verso Press.
Markovitz, Daniel. 2005. Democratic Disobedience. *Yale Law Journal* 114: 1898–1948.
Maynor, John. 2003. *Republicanism is the Modern World*. Malden: Polity Press.
Miller, David. 2012. *National Responsibility and Global Justice*. Oxford: Oxford University Press.
Nagel, Thomas. 2005. The Problem of Global Justice. *Philosophy and Public Affairs* 33(2): 113–147.
Ogunye, Temi. 2015. Global Justice and Transnational Civil Disobedience. *Ethics and Global* 8(1): 27217. doi:10.3402/egp.v8.27217.
Pettit, Philip. 1997. *Republicanism: A Theory of Freedom and Government*. Oxford: Oxford University Press.
Rawls, John. 1971. *A Theory of Justice*. Cambridge, MA: Harvard University Press.
———. 2001. *The Law of Peoples*. Cambridge, MA: Harvard University Press.
———. 2005. *Political Liberalism*. New York: Columbia University Press.
Risse, Mathias. 2015. *On Global Justice*. Princeton: Princeton University Press.
Sabl, Andrew. 2003. Looking Forward to Justice: Rawlsian Civil Disobedience and its Non-Rawlsian Lessons. *Journal of Political Philosophy* 9(3): 307–330.
Scanlon, Thomas Michael. 2000. *What we Owe to Each Other*. Cambridge, MA: Harvard University Press.
Sen, Amartya. 2000. *Development as Freedom*. New York: Doubleday Anchor.
Skinner, Quentin. 2013. *Liberty Before Liberalism*. Cambridge: Cambridge University Press.
Smith, William. 2013. *Deliberative Democracy and Civil Disobedience*. Cambridge: Polity Press.

Chapter 3
Undocumented Disobedients as a Special Class of Civil Disobedients

Abstract In this chapter, I address the status of undocumented global migrants and refugees as justifiably exercising a moral right to disobey, grounded in the international decency standard of the Law of Peoples. They are a special class of disobedients insofar as their everyday acts of participation in the domestic system of cooperation of the country in which they have no legal right of occupancy are obviously disobedient. Nevertheless, these acts do not conform to the established definition to civil disobedience, especially the *publicity* of civilly disobedient acts as condition of their justifiability. Consequently, it becomes necessary to explain why 'undocumented disobedience' is properly a mode of civil disobedience. To this end, I demonstrate that such disobedience is indeed legitimate under the *Law of Peoples*. I argue by analogy with the case of refugees that undocumented migrants are equally vulnerable to the abuses of domination and persecution. In the case of the undocumented, however, they not vulnerable to these abuses in the country they leave, but rather the country they enter without official documentation. In particular, they are vulnerable to overlapping forms of interpersonal and systemic domination and persecution by citizens who exploit their well-founded fear of reporting to the immigration authorities and suffering deportation. I argue that vulnerabilities to domination and persecution, based on exploitation of this fear, establish an urgent human right of the undocumented to protection under the rule of law that violate the principle of reasonable rejection. In this respect, I emphasize that it is already a well-established principle of international law that refugees are entitled to protection of their urgent human rights. This is the principle of non-refoulement: that those seeking refuge from domination and persecution should not suffer returned the countries they have left. Nevertheless, I argue that this principle does not apply to the undocumented, insisting on a normatively relevant between the latter and refugees. That said, however, I argue that peoples owed undocumented *at least* minimal participatory rights in contesting deportation decisions, as a requirement of decency and non-domination. Such contestatory rights are sufficient to overrule the so-

M. Allen, *Civil Disobedience in Global Perspective*,
Studies in Global Justice 16, DOI 10.1007/978-94-024-1164-5_3

called plenary powers of the state to deport non-citizens, absent due process of law, on grounds of protecting the sovereign right of a people to control its own borders.

3.1 Introduction

My purpose in this chapter is to establish that undocumented global migrants constitute a special class of civil disobedients. As a special class of civil disobedients, I define the undocumented first by analogy with refugees. This analogy appeals to the notion of a well-founded fear of persecution based on certain 'protected grounds,' such as race, religion, nationality, political opinion, or membership of a particular group. In the case of refugees, such a fear of persecution *in their home country* is the basis for claiming asylum *in another country*. I argue, however, that undocumented immigrants ought to be recognized under international law as appealing to a well-founded fear of persecution *not* in their home country, but rather in the country in which they presently live, love, and work, without the benefit of formal recognition under domestic laws. In other words, their plight – as undocumented – ought to count as a protected ground, entitling them to some formal legal recognition and protection against persecution in the country whose borders they have crossed absent inspection and permission, as opposed to their home country.

Crossing borders illegally, undocumented immigrants are quite obviously *disobedient*. Nevertheless, their disobedience is not limited to the act of illegal border crossing. It also extends to what I shall call everyday acts of disobedience, such a driving without a license, working without papers, and so on. These everyday acts of disobedience, however, do not align, especially well with the traditional definition of civil disobedience in which disobedient acts, above all, are a mode of public address (Rawls 2001). Publicity distinguishes civil disobedients proper from mere criminals by demonstrating the conscientious nature of their belief that their acts of disobedience expose injustice rather than promote self-interest. Nevertheless, undocumented migrants typically avoid publicity for their disobedient acts. Indeed, fearing detention and deportation, they prefer to remain 'under the radar' of immigration authorities. Such avoidance of publicity might appear to disqualify them as civil disobedients proper. Without publicity, there is no civil disobedience, as opposed to everyday acts of covert resistance to abusive authority. After all, the public character of the act of civil disobedience is an invitation to reconsider current law and policy. Absence of publicity thus undermines the aim of civil disobedience – to bring about a change of law or policy. Consequently, I will have to show why it is appropriate to relax the publicity condition for undocumented disobedients themselves as well as to show how this relaxation is otherwise consistent with satisfying the publicity condition and fulfilling the aim of civil disobedience proper.

Assuming I can do this, however, there should be little doubt that undocumented disobedients can legitimately exercise a moral right to disobey, at least, certain laws of the country whose borders they have crossed without inspection or permission. They may do so inasmuch as they can appeal to moral considerations defeating their duty to obey (Lefkowitz 2007) its laws. In particular, they are subject to overlapping forms of interpersonal and systemic domination that render them a persecuted group within the territorial jurisdiction of the state in which they go about their everyday lives, routinely interacting with its people. Indeed, this phenomenon of internal rather than external domination and persecution constitutes a violation of their urgent human rights, departing from the international decency standard of the *Law of Peoples*. It is a departure from decency insofar as it creates a piecewise injustice (Sabl 2003) within the state between those persons who are and who are not able to access the basic elements of the rule of law, offering protection against domination and persecution. As a function of interpersonal and systemic domination and persecution, such a piecewise injustice targets the undocumented qua undocumented. That is, it targeting them by virtue of their vulnerability as lacking formal legal recognition in the country they have entered illegally, making it impossible to seek protections of domestic law to which they may be entitled without fear of retaliatory reporting to immigration authorities, which may exercise *legitimate sovereign powers* of detention and deportation.

This latter point is central to my analysis of the undocumented as indeed relevantly different from refugees. Non-refoulement properly limits the sovereignty of peoples to decide whom and whom may not cross their borders based on the fundamental moral consideration that *it is indecent to return persons to a situation* of domination and persecution. In the language of the Law of Peoples, non-refoulement is a fundamental requirement of decency. Nevertheless, to the extent the undocumented are not fleeing persecution in another country, it is far from clear that decent peoples owe them any equivalent right not to be deported. Not, at any rate, unless they have a well-founded fear of persecution in their home countries, which case they would properly be refugees, as opposed to undocumented migrants, anyway. Decency, in other words, does not demand that the undocumented *qua* undocumented should enjoy immunity to deportation. Nevertheless, that said, the undocumented may be said to have a well-founded fear of domination and persecution in the country they have entered illegally and *voluntarily*. On a remarkably unsympathetic interpretation of their predicament, it might be argued that the undocumented have not only *chosen to* break the law by crossing borders illegally, but also in doing so they have *chosen to* place themselves in a conditions of domination and persecution. Consequently, their predicament is of their own making and not one of any fundamental injustice *done to them*.

I shall treat this unsympathetic interpretation for what it is worth; that is, *nothing* in terms of fundamental moral analysis. If access to the basic protections of the rule of law is an urgent human right, then the failure of any decent people to secure effective access to the rule of law for everyone within its territorial borders, absent dominating fear of persecution for seeking such protections, amounts to a fundamental moral flaw in its basic institutional arrangements. Peoples owe this sort of protection to the undocumented as a matter of decency, regardless of whether they broke the law in the manner in which they entered the country and regardless of whether their participation in its system of domestic cooperation commits them to everyday disobedient acts. From the standpoint of decency, denial of effective access to the rule of law and its protections against domination and persecution is an injustice done to the undocumented and, as such, justice binds decent peoples to secure for them some legal standing sufficient for non-domination and non-persecution. Crucially, though, justice does no prescribes such a standing premised on their having a right to stay in the country as it is for refugees. Peoples thus owe the undocumented legal protections against internal domination and persecution, but they do not owe the undocumented a right to stay (for an influential collection of discussions on the right to stay, see Carens 2010). In the chapter following this one, I explore in some detail the contents of what decent peoples owe to the undocumented in terms of a human right to be a participant in domestic politics. In this chapter, however, I limit my concerns to laying the groundwork for that claim. Indeed, I (1) clarify the sense in which undocumented disobedients may be understood as civil disobedients proper and (2) make an initial case for the obligations of decent people to secure a legal status for the undocumented sufficient for non-domination and non-persecution within their own territorial borders.

This chapter now proceeds in the following steps. First, I consider undocumented disobedience as a special case of non-citizen disobedience, before exploring the analogue between undocumented and refugees in relation to the ideas of domination and persecution. Second, I consider why undocumented disobedients are not refugees and, third, why they should properly be construed as civil disobedients at all, despite numerous initial difficulties with this designation. Fourth, I consider why the undocumented have a moral right to disobey and introduce a key distinction between external internal and domination, appealing to the overlapping ideas of systemic de jure and de facto domination. Indeed, I also discuss here the potential for conflict between the *justifiable* claims of undocumented disobedients and the so-called plenary power of a government to protect the sovereignty of its people by making immigration decisions, absent due process of law. I then, fifth, dismiss such a power of government as incompatible with decency.

3.2 Undocumented Migration as a Special Case of Non-citizen Civil Disobedience

Before proceeding to the major arguments of the chapter, I begin with an introductory observation that disobedience by the undocumented is a more narrowly conceived version of 'non-citizen disobedience.' This is disobedience undertaken by persons who are *not* citizens of the state whose laws and popular sovereign will they violate. Indeed, non-citizen disobedients hope to re-make those laws in ways that are more consistent with international justice. Nevertheless, their situation differs from that of undocumented migrants in some important respects. For example, non-citizen disobedients may have some recognized legal standing in the country whose laws they break. Such disobedients might enjoy the status of permanent residents. In the context of the US, civil disobedience by permanent residents could potentially result in both detention and *deportation*. It could result in deportation if the laws broken are felonies. To this extent, permanent residents may well face *equivalent* risks to undocumented migrants for conscientiously disobedient acts. Consequently, their situation could be as urgent as that of the undocumented. Moreover, a host people might criticize permanent residents along similar lines to the undocumented for resorting to disobedience. Viz, both attempt to *interfere* in domestic processes of sovereign decision-making that are supposed to be exclusive to citizens.

This much may be true. That is, non-citizen residents may face similar risks to the undocumented and a host people might see non-citizen disobedience generally as an illegitimate form of interference in the sovereign decision-making processes of citizens. Indeed, the latter is interference in the sense that non-citizen do not *leave citizens alone* to make collective decisions regarding the rights and statuses of persons within their territorial jurisdiction, *as they see fit* exercising their sovereign right qua people. Nevertheless, that is certainly not a problem of justice from the standpoint of international decency, under the *Law of Peoples*. It is not a problem to the extent that decency places legitimate constraints on sovereignty by requiring *participatory contestation rights* for all persons, regardless of citizenship. As I argued in the previous chapter, the urgent human right of everyone within the territorial jurisdiction of a state entails participation not in making sovereign decisions (insofar as that remains the sovereign right of citizens), but contesting them by calling for uptake and reconsideration. This means that decent peoples should permit those non-citizens who are aggrieved by a sovereign decision not to demand that it should be overturned (that, again, remains the sovereign right and power of conational citizens), but that it should, at least, be reconsidered and an explanation (Abizadeh 2008) given as to how it satisfies fundamental principles of justice. As a requirement of decency and non-domination, basic contestation rights for non-citizens thus properly limit the claims of all decent peoples to sovereign non-interference.

Nonetheless, there are still important differences between those non-citizens legally recognized as having a right to be in the country and those who have no such recognition. In particular, permanent residents are not vulnerable to the kinds of internal domination and persecution suffered by undocumented migrants. As legally recognized, the former do not suffer the terror of retaliatory reporting for claiming those rights specific to their status in the county or the urgent rights to which all persons are entitled everywhere. That is, legal residents may not be able to claim voting rights or the full range of welfare rights (such as Social Security) to which citizens are entitled, but they are entitled to the full range of civil rights to non-discrimination in housing, employment, education, marriage equality, and so on, in addition to urgent rights of non-servitude and subsistence. To this extent, it might be asserted that there is no, in principle, difference between them and the undocumented in terms of the rights to which they are already entitled. Nevertheless, this is deeply misleading, especially when it comes to the phenomenon of undocumented disobedience.

For legal residents, civil disobedience comes with inherent risks of legal consequences. This might entail a consequence that citizen civil-disobedients never have to face: actual expulsion from the country. Nevertheless, disobedience by legal residents is quite unlike the circumstance of what I shall call ‘everyday’ disobedience characterizing the undocumented, whereby everyday acts of driving unlicensed or working without papers, and so on, expose them to a constant risk of retaliation by unsympathetic or hostile citizens reporting them to the immigration authorities (Ansley 2010). This everyday character of disobedience necessarily creates vulnerabilities to internal domination and persecution from which decent peoples protect legal residents, as I shall argue later in this chapter. Indeed, as inducing fear and even terror (Fernandez and Olsen 2011), such vulnerabilities exclusive to the undocumented provide an initial case for treated them as a special class of non-citizen disobedients. Moreover, as *internal* to the territorial borders of the state, vulnerabilities to domination and persecution should help to clarify my stress on the analogy between the undocumented and refugees.

3.3 The Undocumented Are Not Refugees

There is an obvious comparison between undocumented migrants and refugees. Indeed, both are persons outside their country of origin who have crossed international borders. Nevertheless, from here the comparison with refugees abruptly ends. Broadly understood, undocumented migrants are persons who left their country of origin and crossed international borders, entering another country without inspection or proper permission from its government, or who may have entered it with a legal visa but subsequently remained after that expired. By contrast, refugees are persons who leave their country of origin and cross international borders in order to claim a recognized status under international law (Lister 2013). That is, they cross borders in order to claim the right of asylum in another country, so that its government may properly authorize their presence in that country. Nevertheless, undocumented migrants do not –and cannot – claim any analogous status under law. The obvious, but relevant, difference from 'refugee' is that 'undocumented' is not a legal status legally border crossers may claim from the government of another country. It does not entitle one to stay within its territorial borders or, at least, to be resettled somewhere else that one may enjoy freedom from the dangers one has fled. Instead, it is simply the absence of any status authoring one as having the right to be in the country. To be sure, the lack of such authorization is not a *denial* of other rights in the country that one has entered without documentation and permission. Still the obvious difference here concerning having or not having the legal right to be in the country establishes an entirely different dynamic with its people between refugees and undocumented.

On the one hand, refugees make explicit claims to justice against the people, under the international rule of law, in addition to making explicit appeals to its collective moral conscience. The people indeed encounter refugees as seeking protections of the rule of law that are inaccessible to them in their home countries, in which they suffer persecution on the basis of race, religion, or any other of the protected grounds laid out in the United Nations High Commission for Refugees (UNHCR) 1967 Protocol relating to the Status of Refugees. Here, the deportation of those who can demonstrate well-founded fears of persecution in their home countries would effectively deny them basic rule of law protections demanded by the Law of Peoples. On the other hand, undocumented migrants make neither an explicit claim to justice, grounded in any existing international law, nor explicit appeals to the moral conscience of the people whose society they have surreptitiously entered. In this respect, they make no explicit claim or public appeal that would bar the people by law or by collective moral conscience from deporting them back to their home countries. Of course, the people may still have any number of discretionary reasons not to deport undocumented immigrants (see, for instance, Benton 2010; Carens 2015). But, absent compelling reasons to believe that doing so would effectively deny them the basic protections of the rule of law, deportation cannot be ruled out as a potentially justifiable discretionary judgment of the people; justifiable, that is, as consistent with the decency standard of the Law of Peoples.

These very different dynamics of refugees and undocumented migrants with the people point to whether or not the latter have reason to believe urgent human rights are at risk. Finding reason to believe this to be the case with refugees, the dynamic is fundamentally one of legality and morality defined by the duty of non-refoulement (see Kuosmanen 2014), binding the people by law and conscience not to return them to the country in which they face specifiable risks of persecution. Nevertheless, what reason do the people have to believe that the urgent human rights of undocumented immigrants are at risk? After all, like refugees, undocumented migrants enter a country in which the rule of law is well established. Prima facie, there appear to be no compelling reason to suppose that their urgent human rights to claim its protections are at risk in the country they have entered. Moreover, to the extent they do not claim refugee status, neither is there reason to suppose that their country of origin would deny these rights upon their return. Indeed, no specifiable risk of persecution faces the undocumented and there is nothing approaching the legal and moral clarity of non-refoulement in determining what the people owe to the undocumented.

Nevertheless, the perception of a dynamic based on the people's discretionary judgement, given the absence of any threat to the urgent rights of the undocumented, is misleading at best. It takes little reflection to realize that the dynamic is considerably more complex, pointing instead to obligations rooted in urgency and decency. Not having a legal right to be in the country creates a circumstance in which undocumented migrants are effectively dominated and persecuted *under the rule of law* of a people who are otherwise committed to satisfying the demands of decency. Indeed, the proposition that they face risks of this sort, not in the countries they have left, but the country they have entered, is central to my argument in the section after next that the undocumented are properly civil disobedients. Such risks of persecution faced by the undocumented should count as urgent moral considerations capable of defeating their duty to obey those laws they routinely disobey in that country. Before proceeding to that argument, however, it is first necessary to establish that the undocumented can satisfy certain standard features of the definition of civil disobedience.

3.4 Are the Undocumented Civil Disobedients Proper?

Disobedience that is civil and not merely criminal entails public address, as invitation to deliberate and reconsider existing law and policy (Rawls 2001). Nevertheless, most undocumented avoid publicity, fearing the consequence of deportation. Here, civil disobedience also typically entails a commitment to accepting the legal consequences of disobeying the law, as expression of ongoing fidelity to the principle of law. By avoiding publicity, however, most undocumented try to avoid suffering penalties – again, from fear of deportation (Ansley 2010). Consequently, neither of these two key ingredients of the traditional definition of civil disobedience is present in the case of the undocumented. Does this, then, disqualify the undocumented as civil disobedients? I argue that it does not, and that the publicity and penalties conditions may be relaxed for most undocumented disobedients.

To be sure, there is no need to relax these conditions in the case of some undocumented immigrants, like the participants in the US and Canadian 'undocumented and unafraid' movements. Often brought into the country as infants by their undocumented migrant parents, the participants in these movements demonstrate considerable courage in resorting to traditional forms of civil disobedience, such as disrupting public spaces. Confident in the justice of their cause, well educated, and politically savvy, they publicize their undocumented status, despite the potential consequences of drawing attention to themselves. As 'unafraid,' they conform to the extraordinarily high standards of moral courage for civil disobedients, once insisted upon by Mohandas Gandhi. According to Gandhi (1932), only morally superior persons ought to take on the role of disobedient. Indeed, he saw the moral superiority of disobedients exemplified through their willingness to endure suffering as central to the practical success of disobedience as 'melting the hearts' of oppressors and dominators (Pantham 1982; Sparling 2009; Allen

2015). Most contemporary theorists of civil disobedience (Rawls 2001; Dworkin 1978; Markovitz 2005; Lefkowitz 2007; Lovell 2009; Smith 2013), however, do not endorse Gandhi's heroic notion of the efficacy of self-suffering. Instead, they emphasize the more cognitivist dimensions of disobedience, as motivating critical processes of reconsideration and deliberation through public reason giving. Here, any suffering that may result from the public aspects of civil disobedience plays a much less decisive role than it did in Gandhi.

This more cognitivist emphasis on reason giving need not be dismissive about the moral courage exemplified by undocumented and unafraid or the role it might play in regard to the efficacy of disobedient protest. Nevertheless, it does mean that extraordinary moral courage is not a requirement for the vast majority of understandably fearful undocumented – who avoid publicity and penalties – to qualify as civil disobedients. Indeed, the majority of undocumented immigrants form a class of disobedients defined not by any Gandhian moral superiority and heroism, but rather their very ordinariness. They are not an elite group of self-selecting political activists, choosing a life of extraordinary moral self-sacrifice, bordering on martyrdom. Instead, they are ordinary people trying to go about their workaday lives, without drawing attention to their routine acts of disobeying the law by driving without licenses, working without papers, etc. Regarding the routine, banal nature of their disobedience, their situation is somewhat akin to Partha Chatterjee's (2011) notion of a political society – simultaneously in and outside of civil society – whose members have no practical alternative but to break the law in order to participate in mundane social cooperation. Here, Chatterjee refers to an underclass of impoverished *citizens*, having to resort to petty crime in order to be social participants. By contrast, however, the undocumented are an underclass of *non-citizens* having to break the law in order to conceal their lack of any authorized legal status in the system of cooperation.

In this respect, I use the term everyday disobedience to characterize their situation. Indeed, this may be understood by contrast with everyday *resistance* (Scott 1987), as consisting in acts like foot-dragging as a way to register one's opposition to domination before complying with oppressive laws. An example of this might be, say, a Palestinian from the occupied territory responding only very slowly to the demand of an Israeli soldier to show identity papers (Haugaard 2015). To be sure, an undocumented person driving without a license engages a similar act of resistance to domination, as I shall argue soon. Nevertheless, the latter is not an act of resistance to domination preceding compliance with an oppressive law. Occupying the territory of another people and surveilling the movements of its various members is intrinsically oppressive. There is nothing, however, intrinsically oppressive about requiring drivers should be licensed and insured. Indeed, domination results not from requiring that drivers to be licensed, but from the absence of any documented status that might enable one to legally obtain a license and so comply with an entirely reasonable law. Moreover, everyday disobedience does not entail even the level of publicity involved in everyday resistance. In the above example, the Palestinian foot-dragger makes known his or her opposition to the occupation taunting the soldier with his slow response, before eventually complying. Nevertheless, an undocumented driver in the US is much likelier to deflect and dissemble when confronted by a traffic cop – 'Oh, I'm sorry officer, I must have left my license at home,' 'I must have left it in my other jacket at work,' and the like.

To this extent, everyday undocumented disobedience entails the outright avoidance of any publicity in actually breaking, rather than resentfully complying with, the law. Nevertheless, such disobedience can still indirectly offer an invitation to the people to deliberate and reconsider consistent with civil disobedience. At any rate, this follows on the model of 'assisted disobedience' (Brownlee 2012), whereby surrogates, such as sympathetic public officials and citizens, assume the tasks of publicity on behalf of the undocumented (for a related case of assisted disobedience, see von Essen and Allen 2015). Here, surrogates need not be disobedient themselves, but merely publicize the disobedient acts of others they believe to be justified in disobeying the law, while having sound reasons for wanting to avoid publicity. To be sure, such assistance with publicity would not relieve understandably fearful undocumented disobedients of all of the risks of publicity confronting them. After all, public policy deliberations inevitably draw attention to their situation as everyday disobedients. Nevertheless, it would relieve them of the fear of unwanted attention focused on them *as individuals* by immigration authorities, which might otherwise be the case, if they themselves were to openly seek and embrace publicly like the morally heroic participants in undocumented and unafraid.

What, though, about the penalties requirement? In the case of undocumented and unafraid, the penalties requirement is unproblematic. Here, the appropriate response should be to build a firewall (Carens 2015) between domestic law enforcement generally and immigration law enforcement specifically. This should be a firewall between, on the one hand, law enforcement concerned with processing undocumented disobedients qua civil disobedients and, on the other hand, law enforcement concerned with the enforcement of immigration law. With such a firewall in place, those undocumented engaged in conventional acts of civil disobedience such as sit-ins, or other forms of public obstruction, should suffer the penalties associated with these acts, as public crimes or misdemeanors. Nevertheless, this should not involve any subsequent referral by domestic law enforcement to the immigration authorities. Consequently, undocumented disobedience meets the penalties requirement, but only by virtue of its separation from immigration law enforcement. Nonetheless, the penalties requirement obviously remains problematic in the case of those undocumented of ordinary, as opposed to extraordinary, moral courage, who seek to avoid penalties entirely by avoiding publicity for their everyday acts of disobedience.

After all, the latter might still suffer the penalties for driving without a license, for instance, even if the firewall ensures that accountability for driving unlicensed could not result in any subsequent referral to the immigration authorities. That would relieve them of their greatest and most oppressive fear: detention and deportation. Nevertheless, it would not remove their motivation to continue avoiding the penalties for their everyday disobedient acts, as much as they can. It would not do so inasmuch as they would still be motivated to perform these acts. Indeed, their ability to function within the system of cooperation depends on their ability to continue driving unlicensed, work without papers, etc. Absent any more comprehensive policy responses to address the problems they face as undocumented, they would necessarily retain their motivation to disobey, while also seeking to avoid future penalties and publicity. Is it, then appropriate that the penalties requirement be relaxed in their case so that they may nonetheless qualify as civil disobedients proper? I answer yes. After all, it is excessive and inappropriate to demand that persons of merely ordinary moral courage rise to the level of superior Gandhian moral courage.

Indeed, this highlights the difference between the vast majority of undocumented today and the vast majority of Black Americans living under Jim Crow laws in the 1950s. For most Black Americans, during that time, a practical alternative to disobedience was simply to go about their workaday lives and obey unjust racial segregation laws, thus denying law enforcement any credible reason for singling them out. They could then look to their more morally courageous peers to accept and suffer the legal consequences of flouting Jim Crow by, say, drinking at the 'Whites Only' water fountain. Here, the leadership of the American Civil Rights movement certainly never advocated that the vast majority of Black Americans under Jim Crow should resort to civil disobedience. The leadership would have surely rejected any such proposition, even though all Black Americans had a moral right to disobey Jim Crow (Sabl 2003). Indeed, calling for such universal civil disobedience would have placed an entirely unreasonable demand on the majority of ordinary persons, trying to get by in a circumstance of fundamental injustice.

Of course, by contrast with Black Americans in the 1950s, the undocumented do not have the same option of simply going about their ordinary lives in compliance with law. That is actually beside the point as far as a demand for moral heroism is concerned. By parity of reasoning, any demand for such heroism through universal civil disobedience would be equally unreasonable in the case of the vast majority of ordinary undocumented persons going about their workaday lives. That is, going about their lives under different circumstances of injustice defined not by oppressive laws, like Jim Crow, but rather the lack of a legal right to be in the country. Consequently, it ought to be acceptable that most undocumented are relieved of this excessive and inappropriate moral demand by assistance from surrogates and the morally courageous acts of undocumented peers, willing to engage in more traditional acts of civil disobedience, such as the activists of undocumented and unafraid. Relieved of this excessive and inappropriate demand for moral heroism, the undocumented are thus properly civil disobedients. Indeed, they are disobedient in virtue of being in the country without having any legal right to be there, unlike Black Americans of ordinary rather than extraordinary moral courage living under Jim Crow. Nevertheless, they are also *civilly* disobedient to the extent that surrogates present their disobedience to the people as a call to reconsider, according to the model of assisted disobedience.

3.5 Why the Undocumented Have a Moral Right to Disobey: Internal Domination and Persecution

It is now incumbent on me to defend my proposition from the section before last that the undocumented face risks of domination and persecution not the countries they have left, but in the country they have entered whose people is otherwise committed to satisfying the demands of decency. Such a society guarantees urgent human rights of access to the basic elements of the rule of law not only for its own citizens, but also for refugees whose urgent rights may at risk in their home countries. Nevertheless, it does not effectively guarantee such access for the undocumented. To this extent, the undocumented may rightly appeal to their experience of internal domination and persecution as basic moral considerations defeating their duty to obey (Lefkowitz 2007). Consistent with my argument from Chapter One, these considerations both justify their disobedience and place the people who are the addressees of their claims to justice – as delivered directly or by surrogates – under a binding obligation of uptake and reconsideration that cannot reasonably be rejected (Scanlon 2000).

I begin then by exploring the idea of domination in relation to the undocumented, before elaborating this in terms of the phenomenon of internal persecution. The idea of domination, at first, might not appear to be an especially good fit when applied to the undocumented. Not, at any rate, when they experience injustice in an otherwise decent society with strong commitments to the rule of law. Indeed, in its broadest sense, domination may be said to consist in being subjected to an arbitrary power that cannot be effectively challenged (Pettit 1997). This may be interpreted as an arbitrary interpersonal power, as in the case of the highway robber who dominates his victims by threatening them at gunpoint 'Your money or your life.' Here, law neither sanctions domination nor does it have any backing in the norms and expectations of the wider social system. Nevertheless, most cases of domination happen under the color of law and right (Richardson 2003; also see Blunt 2015). In the ante-bellum Southern US, for instance, the slaveholder's power to exercise an arbitrary will over the slave had the normative backing of the lawful institution of slave holding, as well as established social conventions regarding the justifiability of human bondage. In other words, by contrast with the highwayman case, ante-bellum slavery had the *de jure* backing of law and *de facto* backing of such conventions. The highway robber always acted against the law and subject to widespread social censure. Nevertheless, not only could the slaveholder exercise the power of domination over the slave not only without threat of legal consequences and moral censure. The latter also could continue exercising this power with impunity because of the systemic backing of law and convention. Consequently, domination is a systemic and not merely interpersonal power.

What does this distinction between interpersonal and systemic modes of domination tell us, though, about the undocumented? Their situation is one of having *no authorized status* under the rule of law that otherwise governs the society in which they cooperate with all those who do have such a status, as citizens, legal residents, and so on. To this extent, however, their circumstance is not analogous to slaves subjected to arbitrary interpersonal interference from powerful individuals *who have the backing of law*. Indeed, there is no de jure sanction to the domination of the undocumented. On the contrary, the undocumented ostensibly enjoy protection from a substantive range of anti-discrimination laws, for instance, in employment and housing, which apply to *all persons* within the territorial jurisdictions of the US. Moreover, they are ostensibly enjoy such protection from the criminal law generally. To this extent, the legal system ought to protect them from discrimination as arbitrary interpersonal interference from powerful individuals, ranging from unscrupulous employers and landlords, seeking to take advantage of them, to the highwayman threatening 'Your money or your life.' Nonetheless, the undocumented are still highly vulnerable to domination as arbitrary interpersonal interference. They are subjected to such dominating interference, again, from employers or landlords ignoring employment or housing regulations, corrupt police officers hustling brides, xenophobic service providers simply refusing service and so on (Ansley 2010). Nevertheless, this is arbitrary interpersonal interference not with the backing of law, but rather *despite* the de jure protections ostensibly afforded them by the non-arbitrary rule of law. It is also *despite* the de facto conventions of a people committed to respect for all persons as moral equals, repudiating the categorization of certain persons as moral inferiors whom it is permissible to exploit.

In this respect, their circumstance is clearly not one of de jure domination but rather a peculiar circumstance of domination that arises in spite of de jure protections and de facto background conventions. I call this domination by virtue of *conditional statuslessness* by contrast with statelessness (Arendt 2011). Indeed, the idea of stateless persons is a familiar paradigm of domination. Here, statelessness denotes a condition of absolute and global vulnerability to domination, not having any recognized legal status in any sovereign community capable of enforcing urgent human rights. Such absolute, global vulnerability gives rise to the right to have rights, which translates into the right to be the member of some decent rights-respecting community capable of such enforcement. To be sure, there is a sense in which stateless persons are also undocumented persons: after all, a state*less* person will not even has a passport. Nevertheless, this still does not describe the vast majority of cases of undocumented persons who are already members of states and indeed states that are decent in the sense of protecting the urgent human rights of citizens and residents. In light of my earlier contrast with refugees, undocumented persons have left their home countries not because they are fleeing persecution but because they are responding to various pressures of globalization. To this extent, not only do they have the status of being the bearers of certain rights in the country whose borders they have crossed, without the permission of its people, in responding to such pressures. They also may have the status of being members of a state whose people indeed conform to the international decency standard. Nonetheless, they are conditionally statusless in the sense that they do not have a legal right to be *where they are.*

Such conditional statuslessness by virtue of not having the legal right to be where they are produces the peculiar phenomenon of *de facto acquiescence* to domination. That is, the undocumented by custom or habit do not seek the protections of the non-arbitrary rule of law to which they are already entitled. Such custom or habit is a function of their entirely understandable fear of the potential legal consequences of seeking such protections, as previously discussed. Here, there is little doubt that citizens as interpersonal dominators can take advantage of the undocumented by imposing their arbitrary will upon them by virtue of the threat of retaliatory reporting to immigration authorities for non-compliance with their exploitative demands. To be sure, the threat of retaliatory reporting is not equivalent to the highwayman threatening one's life. Nonetheless, the structure of domination otherwise replicates the highwayman case in at least some important ways. The highwayman relies on the de facto acquiesce of his victims. The norm of conduct in that situation is to comply with the highwayman's exploitative demand, rather than resort to heroics potentially endangering one's life or the lives of one's fellow travelers. That the travelers routinely, or conventionally, acquiesce by handing over their money does nothing to diminish the circumstance as one of domination. Nevertheless, while he is at odds with the law, the highwayman expects his victims to demand ex ante legal protection against his criminal activity and seek ex post facto legal redress for his crimes. That said, however, the relationship between undocumented and citizens as interpersonal dominators is quite different. The latter not only rely on the former's habit or custom of acquiescence to exploitative demands, but also on their habit or custom of *not* demanding protection or redress under the rule of law. In this respect, it might even be said that de facto acquiesce to domination in the case of the undocumented is closer to the case of the gangster running a protection racket than to the highway robber. Viz., citizen dominators of the undocumented do not say 'your money or your life,' but rather 'I'll protect you from detention and deportation, by not reporting you to the immigration authorities, only if you acquiesce to my demands.'

Moreover, the expectation of de facto acquiescence to domination by undocumented of merely ordinary moral courage is quite unlike the slavery case: indeed, contrary to slavery, the law does not actually *license* the domination of anyone within the territorial jurisdiction of the state. Domination, again, manifests itself through the habit or custom of acquiescence to threats against which the rule of law offers no effective protections. In summary, then, my claim is that the undocumented are dominated on the model of de facto acquiesce to domination owing to their conditional statuslessness as lacking the right to be where they are. Indeed, such acquiescence to domination results from the fear of retaliatory reporting and the potential for deportation. Nevertheless, if lacking the right to be where they are results in their internal domination and persecution, then the undocumented cannot legitimately claim anything like a right to stay where they are, or right of non-refoulement equivalent to that legitimately enjoyed by refugees. Not any rate, if peoples are to retain sovereign rights of border controls. To be sure, this sovereign right of peoples is not absolute. Sovereignty is constrained by decency and urgent human rights. Indeed, these constraints mean that the non-refoulement rights of refugees are binding insofar as it is reasonable to expect deportation will result in violations of such rights in their home countries. Nevertheless, as I have already argued, there is no equivalent violation of the decency and urgency standards when it comes to deporting the undocumented insofar as there is no reasonable expectation – on any of the special grounds laid out by the UNHCR – of that resulting in external domination and persecution abroad.

This, then, raises the question of what the principle of reasonable rejection applied to decent peoples entails in the case of the undocumented, if not a right to be where they are, a right to stay. I answer that question in the following chapter. The next section of this chapter, however, I explore the parameters of reasonable rejection in relation to the undocumented in light of the doctrine of the plenary power of governments to decide immigration cases, independently of due process and judicial review (Mendoza 2011). Not only is it infeasible for the plenary powers doctrine to be reconciled with my preceding analysis of the undocumented as internally dominated. The rigorous and systematic application of the doctrine would also result in a quite different mode of domination from de facto acquiescence to the exploitative demands of citizens: systemic de jure domination by the state. Nonetheless, I argue that the illegitimacy of the plenary powers doctrine from the standpoint of decency and urgent human rights helps to clarify exactly what decent peoples owe to those global migrants who have no legal right to be where they are.

3.6 The Plenary Powers Doctrine and Uptake for Dissent and Contestation

In the context of US constitutionalism, the plenary power of government derives from a couple of nineteenth-century Supreme Court rulings, never revisited and overturned. These rulings assert that the due process of law has no application the government's exclusion and expulsion decisions. To this extent, the rulings of the Supreme Court of the United States (SCOTUS) might well appear to be simultaneously a case of domination and a violation of decency. After all, the SCOTUS rulings purport to justify the systematic denial to those importantly affected (Gould 2013) by the sovereign decisions of government access to a basic element of the rule of law in the legal guarantee of uptake for dissent and contestation, appealing to fundamental principles of justice. Nonetheless, the SCOTUS emphatically denied that its plenary power to decide immigration cases is any power of domination. In this respect, it contended that exclusion or expulsion is neither punishment for a crime nor banishment, but simply a method of enforcing repatriation for non-citizens who have failed to comply with conditions of residency determined by the national government acting in the name of the people.

Indeed, the SCOTUS further contended that any assertion to the contrary – defending the due process rights of non-citizens – would effectively deny the sovereign independence of the nation state, rendering it subject to the control of another power. Nevertheless, it is, at best, hyperbolic, to say that undocumented migrants crossing borders in search of, say, economic opportunities for their families are 'another power,' threating the sovereign independence of the nation and its people. The undocumented do not officially or, for that matter, unofficially represent another sovereign people. Moreover, it is a category mistake to confuse diverse undocumented migrant populations, from many different countries, with any singular people. The is further accentuated, if it is assumed that each nationality of undocumented immigrants represents a *different* sovereign threat from a *different* people, aspiring to control the nation and people with whom they interact. Consequently, I dismiss any idea that the undocumented pose a threat to nation and people in the sense of domination or subjection to another sovereign power.

Nevertheless, even if the undocumented do not dominate the people among whom they interact, the reverse claim that the people dominate the undocumented has genuine credibility. Regarding the government's plenary power, domination becomes a function of the state's rigorous and systematic application of the law, rather than citizens making exploitative demands confident that their victims will not seek legal protections even though protections are available. Call this systemic de jure domination. This mode of domination amounts to an idealized version of apartheid in which racist judges impartially apply unjust racial segregation laws (Blunt 2015). Such an idealized version of apartheid is systematic to the extent there is purportedly no trace of arbitrariness in the decisions of the racist judges. Nevertheless, it is still domination in the sense of the *non-arbitrary* or systematic application of *unjust law*. In contrast with this notion of idealized apartheid, however, the plenary power of government is not domination in the sense of sense of immigration officials systematically applying *unjust* law. Indeed, as I have argued all along by way of distinguishing the undocumented from refugees, immigration law permitting the deportation of undocumented persons is not inherently unjust or indecent, in the manner of apartheid or Jim Crow laws.

If it is a mode of systemic de jure domination – which I believe it that it is – then the government's exercise of its plenary power is domination by virtue of laws that are, in principle, morally justifiable. Why, then, should the plenary powers doctrine be thought to entail any mode of domination whatsoever, if the government's deportation decisions *could be* defended according to fundamental principles of justice? The answer is simple enough. It is *in*sufficient for non-domination to say that officials could defend such decisions, according to these principles. That is, it is insufficient that they could defend their decisions to one another as equally impartial, absent any public mechanisms of dissent and contestation by those who subjected to their systematic application and enforcement. Non-domination depends, above all, on the idea of standing as a legal person (Pettit 1997; Bohman 2007). This means more than treatment in accordance with justice by an ideally impartial government official as superannuated philosopher king. Being a legal person means having the right to call for peoples to reconsider sovereign decisions, in light of fundamental principles of justice, such that government officials are placed under a binding obligation of uptake. Crucially, under the Law of Peoples, there is a binding obligation of uptake even to those persons who have no right to be where they are. Domination is ultimately a denial of standing and any possibility of effective legal redress under the rule of law; a clear violation of international decency standards. It would thus be unreasonable for any decent people to deny standing sufficient for non-domination to any persons whether or not they have a legal right to be within its territorial jurisdiction.

Here, the binding character of the government's obligation of uptake to anyone it subjects to its laws may be supported in two separate but related ways. On the one hand, the ideal of systematic impartiality is impractical. In the decidedly non-ideal world of actual decision-making and enforcement, the implicit or explicit biases of government officials will almost inevitably obtrude, or officials may become unprincipled and corrupt, bending to tyrannical majoritarian opinion or special financial interests. Due process and contestation are thus practical necessities for challenging the biases and corruption of officials, ensuring that decisions and enforcement remain consistent with underlying principles for the legitimacy of law. On the other hand, they are also a necessary condition of law's legitimacy, appealing to the moral equality of persons as legal subjects. The fundamental condition of moral equality, under the Law of Peoples, is that all persons subject to law are entitled to an explanation and justification for its application and enforcement. Nevertheless, this indeed clarifies what decent peoples owe to the undocumented. They owe them precisely what the plenary powers doctrine denies: uptake for dissent and contestation grounded in the fundamental principles of justice endorsed by decent peoples. At a minimum, uptake entails due process of law in deportation cases. Nevertheless, this alone does not address the mode of domination to which I have argued the undocumented are most vulnerable. Not systemic de jure domination, but rather domination by way of de facto acquiescence to exploitative demands made by citizens who are confident that the latter will not claim rights and protections to which they are already entitled.

How, then, is this mode of internal domination to be addressed? What is required for non-domination in the case of undocumented subjects of law who decline claiming its protections? Indeed, another way to ask this question is to ask what *changes*, at the level of domestic law and policy, are appropriate for decent peoples to entertain in response to what I have called in this chapter justifiable everyday undocumented civil disobedience. In the following chapter, I shall argue that a people's obligation of uptake for dissent and contestation by the undocumented entails recognizing and protecting their urgent human right to be participants in the domestic politics of the country in which they have no legal right to have entered or to remain.

3.7 Conclusion

The purpose of this chapter has been to defend the idea that undocumented migrants are a special class of civil disobedients from the objection that they fail to satisfy the definition of civil disobedients. I have argued against this objection that undocumented disobedience is civil disobedience proper, granting the validity of assisted disobedience and the inappropriateness of demands for moral heroism. Undocumented migrants suffer forms of interpersonal and systemic domination in domestic cooperation violating decency. Overcoming these violations entails that all decent peoples recognize the urgent rights of the undocumented to participate appropriately in domestic politics. Indeed, the moral obligation of decent peoples to recognize such rights follows from the principle of reasonable rejection. Nevertheless, the sovereignty rights of decent peoples to national self-determination, in light of their collective moral character, must be reconciled with their recognizing an urgent human right to political participation for undocumented migrants, as I discuss next.

References

Abizadeh, Arash. 2008. Democratic Theory and Border Coercion: No Right to Unilaterally Control Your Own Borders. *Political Theory* 36(1): 37–65.

Allen, Michael. 2015. Truth and Reasonableness in Gandhi and Rawls: *Satyagraha* Without Suffering? *Journal of Indian Philosophy and Religion* 20: 66–93.

Ansley, Fran. 2010. *Constructing Citizenship without a License. Studies in Social Justice* 4(2): 165–170.

Arendt, Hannah. 2011. *Origins of Totalitarianism.* Charleston: Nabu Press.

Benton, Meghan. 2010. The Tyranny of the Enfranchised Majority? The Accountability of States to their Non-Citizen Population. *Res Publica* 16: 397–413.

Blunt, Gwilym. 2015. On the Source, Sites, and Modes of Domination. *Journal of Political Power* 8(1): 5–20.

Bohman, James. 2007. *Democracy Without Borders.* Cambridge, MA: The MIT Press.

Brownlee, Kimberley. 2012. *Conscience and Conviction: The Case for Civil Disobedience.* Oxford: Oxford University Press.

Carens, Joseph. 2010. *The Ethics of Immigration.* Cambridge, MA: The MIT Press.

———. 2015. *The Ethics of Immigration.* Oxford: Oxford University Press.

Chatterjee, Partha. 2011. *Lineages of Political Society: Studies in Post-Colonial Culture.* New York: Columbia University Press.

Dworkin, Ronald. 1978. *Taking Rights Seriously.* Cambridge, MA: Harvard University Press.

Fernandez, Luis, and Joel Olsen. 2011. *To Live Love and Work Anywhere You Please. Contemporary Political Philosophy* 10: 412–418.

Gandhi, Mohandas. 1932. *Yervada Mandir.* Trans. V.G. Desai. Ahmedabad: Navjivan.

Gould, Carol. 2013. The Human Right to Democracy and its Global Import. In *Human Rights: The Hard Cases*, ed. Cindy Holder and David Reidy. Cambridge: Cambridge University Press.

Haugaard, Mark. 2015. Reflections upon Empowerment/Domination Social Change and the Four Dimensions of Power. *Journal of Political Power* 8(1): 293–297.

Kuosmanen, Jaakko. 2014. *What's So Special About Persecution? Ethical Theory and Moral Practice* 17: 129–140.

Lefkowitz, David. 2007. On a Moral Right to Civil Disobedience. *Ethics* 117(2): 202–233.

Lister, Matthew. 2013. Who Are Refugees? *Law and Philosophy* 32: 645–671.

Lovell, James. 2009. *Crimes of Dissent: Civil Disobedience, Criminal Justice and the Politics of Conscience.* New York: New York University Press.

Markovitz, Daniel. 2005. Democratic Disobedience. *Yale Law Journal* 114: 1898–1948.

Mendoza, Jose. 2011. Neither a State of Nature nor a State of Emergency: Law, Sovereignty, and Immigration. *Radical Philosophy Review* 14(2): 187–195.

Pantham, Thomas. 1982. Habermas' Practical Discourse and Gandhi's Satyagraha. *Praxis International* 2: 190–205.

Pettit, Philip. 1997. *Republicanism: A Theory of Freedom and Government.* Oxford: Oxford University Press.

Rawls, John. 2001. *The Law of Peoples.* Cambridge, MA: Harvard University Press.

Richardson, Henry. 2003. *Democratic Autonomy: Public Reasoning about the Ends of Policy.* Oxford: Oxford University Press.

Sabl, Andrew. 2003. Looking Forward to Justice: Rawlsian Civil Disobedience and its Non-Rawlsian Lessons. *Journal of Political Philosophy* 9(3): 307–330.

Scanlon, Thomas Michael. 2000. *What We Owe to Each Other*. Cambridge, MA: Harvard University Press.

Scott, James. 1987. *Weapons of the Weak*. New Haven: Yale University Press.

Smith, William. 2013. *Deliberative Democracy and Civil Disobedience*. Cambridge: Polity Press.

Sparling, Robert. 2009. M. K. Gandhi: Reconciling Agonism and Deliberative Democracy. *Representations* 45(4): 391–404.

Von Essen, Erica, and Michael Allen. 2015. Reconsidering Illegal Hunting as a Crime of Dissent: Implications for Justice and Deliberative Uptake. *Criminal Law and Philosophy* 1(16): 213–228.

Chapter 4
Institutionalizing the Human Right of the Undocumented to Be Domestic Political Participants

Abstract In the previous chapter, I argued for the justifiability of undocumented disobedience. I also argued that decent peoples owe the undocumented disobedients immunity to deportation proceedings initiated specifically in response to their justifiable civilly disobedient acts. This is to acknowledge a *moral* right of undocumented migrants to participate in the domestic politics of the country in which they have no *legal* right to live, love, and work. Is there, however, a legal right that may be said to be owed to undocumented migrants in virtue of the justifiability of their disobedient protest? I argue next that there should be such a legal right. Nevertheless, this is not a right to become a citizen or a right to stay or not to be deported. Instead, it is a right of global undocumented migrants to demand that decent peoples formally recognize and protect them *as political participants* in shaping and influencing the sovereign decisions of the people of which they are not members. This requires embedding such a right to be a political participant, wherever one is, in the institutional arrangements of all decent societies, both democratic and hierarchical. In this respect, I argue that it is actually the key institutional feature of Rawls' concept of the decent hierarchical society – the consultation procedure representing the interests of groups with differentially distributed rights – that provides the most appropriate forum for institutionalizing a human right to be a participant, wherever one is and wherever one is from. Indeed, such non-democratic procedures of consultation and representation may be adapted to the context of minimally democratic societies.

4.1 Introduction

My concern, then, in this chapter is not with justifying the moral right of the undocumented to be disobedient. Instead, it is to ask what kind of legal reform should be the primary aim of such disobedience. Here, an intuitive way to think about legal reform in relation to undocumented disobedience is

M. Allen, *Civil Disobedience in Global Perspective*,
Studies in Global Justice 16, DOI 10.1007/978-94-024-1164-5_4

as reform of immigration policy. That is, undocumented disobedients and their allies aim at promoting some path to citizenship or some alternative version of a right to stay. This is not, however, where I choose to focus my discussion. My argument so far has been that the undocumented are especially vulnerable to domination and internal persecution. Consequently, their most urgent need is for an appropriate legal status capable of effectively guaranteeing protection against these harms; that is, a legal status *other than* a citizenship or non-refoulement. Nevertheless, I have also argued that domination and internal persecution provide a basis of moral considerability that is sufficiently strong to override any absolutist claim of the state to sovereignty in exercising a plenary power over immigration. This latter point now becomes important in that it offers a first step towards conceptualizing an obligation of the state to recognize and institutionally embed a legal status for undocumented migrants necessary to enable them to protect themselves against these harms.

Indeed, the plenary powers doctrine falsely assumed that sovereignty is under assault (Ansley 2010) by anything other than absolute control over borders and the right to deport migrants absent due process and judicial review. Nevertheless, the alternative notion of the state as possessing only a *presumptive* right of such control corrects this false view (Wellman and Cole 2011; Walzer 1984). In contrast with the plenary powers doctrine, the state's merely presumptive right to control immigration and make deportation decisions is decidedly *non-absolutist*. On this view, the state is legitimate in exercising its right to control cross-border movement only on the presumption that it honors the basic human rights of all individual persons, without regard to national memberships. This means that the legitimacy presumption goes *in favor of* those human-rights claimants over whom the state exercises such power and, as such, *against* the state. The basis for this presumption is an acknowledgement that the state is an inherently coercive institution. Consequently, the state is always *under an obligation* to justify its uses of sovereign power to all those it places under coercion, citizen or non-citizen (Abizadeh 2008). My argument from here is that this legitimacy presumption obliges the state to embed a human right of undocumented migrants to be participants in shaping the sovereign domestic political decisions in its basic institutional arrangements.

I develop this argument by appealing first to the plight of undocumented migrants in the United States (for a related discussion of the undocumented as legitimate political subjects in Europe as well as the United States, see Nicholls 2013). In particular, I appeal to the case study of SB 1070, as a piece of citizen-initiated legislation in the US state of Arizona designed to render insecure the rights of undocumented migrants; that is, render insecure (Benton 2010) rights of due process and non-discrimination that the US federal government is obliged to protect. Here, the federal government of the US formally acknowledges the standards of decency and non-domination as applied to the undocumented. Nevertheless, by the activism of nativist citizens reacting to their (false) perceptions of lost sovereignty jeopardize these standards, along with the international legitimacy of the US. Indeed, this poses a human-rights threat to undocumented migrants. Countering this threat entails equipping them with the institutional means to protect their rights to non-domination and non-persecution as participants in the basic institutional structure of US society. Although this argument from the insecurity of rights appeals to a case study of the undocumented in the US, the same kind of insecurity for the undocumented would emerge in the Rawls' hypothetical case of hierarchical societies. Insecurity with respect to those rights owed to the undocumented is a function of the asymmetry of political power between them and citizens. On the one hand, the former guaranteed access to the basic institutions through which they reach sovereign legislative-decisions while, on the other hand, the former excluded from participation in these institutions.

My claim, then, in this chapter is that the undocumented can only secure their rights through participation in the basic structure of institutions for decent societies. Nevertheless, this points to a deep question in political theory concerning the relationship between human rights and political participation. What is their relationship? Are human rights independent of political participation or are human rights and political participation interdependent on one another? Moreover, if the relationship is one of functional independency, what kind of political participation is required for human rights? Does decency prescribe that political participation should be equated with a human right to democracy, in the minimalist sense of participation by citizens in universal suffrage equal voting rights? Alternatively, does it prescribe the *interdependency* of political participation with human rights, quite *independently* of democracy? I shall argue for a version of the latter option. That is, I argue that there is a substantial relationship of interdependence between human rights and *non-democratic* political participation. In this respect, I appeal to the model of participation in basic institutions, absent universal suffrage and equal voting rights, characteristic of decent hierarchical societies, as conceived by Rawls (2001).

I proceed in the following steps. I first briefly consider the interrelationship between human rights and political participation, in light of the presumption against the state and in favor of all those placed under its powers of coercion. Second, I turn to the case study of SB 1070 in order to establish that political participation by the undocumented is coextensive with the realization of their human rights. Third, I argue for recognition and protection of an urgent human right to be a political participant, wherever one is. Fourth, I consider the possibilities for embedding such a novel human right in the basic institutional arrangements of both democratic and hierarchical societies by appeal to the idea of fiduciary or trustee representation. Fifth, I offer a proposal for interpreting such representation in terms of hierarchical mini-publics.

4.2 Interdependency of Human Rights and Political Participation

The presumptive right of the state to control immigration appeals to the legitimation standard of human rights. Nevertheless, it is feasible to conceive of human rights independently of political participation. In the *Law of Peoples* (Rawls 2001), human rights constitute a special class of urgent rights, such as non-servitude and subsistence. To be sure, these rights presuppose that citizens possess capacities and opportunities for political participation in the basic institutional arrangements of decent societies, whether democratic or hierarchical. Nevertheless, Rawls does not present such participation itself as human right. Neither does he conceive of the political participation rights of non-citizens with no legal right to be in the country. Nor, for that matter, does he address the question of whether the state has any obligation to create institutional provisions allowing those without a legal right to be in the country to claim such rights. That said, however, it is surely *implicit* to the *Law of Peoples* that there is some kind of interdependency relationship between the realization of human rights and political participation. After all, Rawls clearly takes the institutionalization of citizens' contestations and ongoing dissent to be fundamental conditions of legitimacy and decency. Indeed, meeting urgent human rights standards, like non-servitude and subsistence, presupposes citizens exercising capacities and opportunities of dissent, which are legally recognized and embedded in the institutional structures of all decent societies.

Nevertheless, contrary to Rawls, some advocates for global justice quite explicitly develop an interdependency relationship between human rights and political participation, insisting upon its close tie to democracy, in the minimalist sense of universal suffrage and voting among the collective body of citizens who make up a people. For instance, the satisfaction of minimal human rights is a condition for citizens exercising democratic rights of participation. As regards an urgent human right to subsistence, starving citizens may be too weak to make it to the voting booth. On this account, the satisfaction of urgent human rights is lexically prior to the realization of democracy and universal suffrage (Riker 2014). Alternatively, human rights and democracy are interrelated insofar as universal suffrage and voting ensures that government officials must be responsive to the people, securing its most urgent needs and interests (Sen 2000). Further, human rights and democracy are *coextensive* (Shue 1996; Christiano 2013; Reidy 2012): non-servitude and subsistence can no more be enjoyed without democratic political participation than the latter enjoyed without the satisfaction of such rights. Hence, human rights and democracy thus go hand in glove. On each of these accounts, human right entail a strong connection to political participation, *as minimally democratic*. Nonetheless, the requirement of minimal democracy amounts to an unduly limited conception of political participation, given the implicit interdependency of human rights and non-democratic political participation in *Law of Peoples*.

Indeed, the co-extensiveness of human rights and minimal democracy (1) fails to capture the idea of a similar interdependency relationship in non-democratic, decent hierarchical societies and (2) it has nothing to say about the question of an interdependency relationship between political participation by those who have not right to be in a country and the realization of their urgent rights. Before addressing the interdependency of political participation and urgent human rights in (1) and (2), however, I turn to my case study of SB 1070. Here, my concern is with clarifying the need for undocumented migrants to become political participants in order to secure those rights to which they are already entitled in a decent society. Clarifying this need, I argue for adding political participation by the undocumented to the special category of urgent human rights articulated in the *Law of Peoples*. I add it to this list insofar as it is coextensive with securing those other rights falling into the category of urgent rights. In particular, I argue that political participation by the undocumented is coextensive with realizing their urgent rights to non-domination and non-persecution.

4.3 The Insecurity of Rights, and Power-Asymmetries Between Citizens and the Undocumented

Citizen activism makes vivid the need for undocumented migrants to become political participants. Indeed such activism renders insecure the urgent rights of the undocumented to non-domination and non-persecution, even when the state itself is committed to satisfying the human rights presumption of legitimacy. The contents and meanings of rights is always a function of political participation in complex processes of negotiation (Arat 2006; Benton 2010). These processes, however, assume that the participants are citizens guaranteed a secure basis of power from which to influence negotiations, without fear of domination or persecution. Consequently, there is always a "gap" between the rights of citizens and non-citizens, "in quality if not quantity:" the rights of the latter are never altogether *settled* but "often criticized, discussed, debated or altered in the course of public debate in a way that citizen's rights are not" (Benton 2010, 400). Here, the unsettled and insecure status of the rights of non-citizens without the right to be in the country, like the undocumented is especially acute. Indeed, it is acute insofar as it leaves the door open to a reprise of de facto domination and internal persecution, despite the door to systemic de jure domination having been closed by the state's embracing the legitimacy presumption of human rights.

This phenomenon can be seen in Arizona's 2010 'Support Our Law Enforcement and Safe Neighborhoods Act,' or SB 1070. As motivated by nativist anxieties about globalization and the supposed threat that undocumented migrants pose to sovereignty (Fernandez and Olsen 2011), the stated purpose of SB 1070 is "to make attrition through enforcement the public policy of all state and local government agencies in Arizona." This is accomplished through requiring law enforcement to check the immigration status of persons they may "reasonably suspect" are undocumented based on factors such as language, accent, clothing, hairstyle, foreign birth, proximity to the border, nervousness, and furtive behavior. Moreover, SB 1070 made it a crime to "transport, move, conceal, harbor or shield" any undocumented persons if one "knows or recklessly disregards" that they are undocumented, and empowered citizens to sue municipalities they believe are not enforcing these provisions. Consequently, it sought to empower Arizona citizens to demand that state and local government *take from the federal US government* the leading role in shaping immigration policy.

Such a policy of attrition through the enforcement of local public policy *effectively substitutes* for the plenary power of the federal government to deport undocumented migrants. That is, it substitutes for this arbitrary systemic power at the federal level of national self-government to the extent that it induces "enough fear and terror" of ongoing harassment by law enforcement "that one chooses to go away," saving the federal government the expense and effort of deportation (Fernandez and Olsen 2011, p. 415). Indeed, the climate of intimidation created by SB 1070 extends even to "documented people who associate with undocumented people or who simply refuse to turn them in" (Ibid). This subjects the undocumented – and perhaps even some documented – to what I called, in the previous chapter, de facto domination and internal persecution. That is, it subjects them to domination through intimidation and fear, regardless of legal protections formally extended to them at the federal level of government. These formal protections range from the urgent human rights, articulated in the *Law of Peoples*, to civil non-discrimination rights. Hence, the attrition policies characteristic of SB 1070 are clearly at odds with the US federal government being able to maintain its claim to international legitimacy, under the decency standard of the Law of Peoples. At any rate, this is true if decency entails non-domination and non-persecution, as I have argued all along.

In the case of SB1070, the US federal government responded to Arizona's indecent attrition policies of creating local conditions of domination and internal persecution. Indeed, the SCOTUS struck down key parts of SB 1070 in a 5-3 ruling in 2012. This ruling denied that Arizona could make it a state misdemeanor for an immigrant not to be carrying documentation of lawful presence in the country, or that state police could perform arrests without a warrant in some situations. It also denied that Arizona could make it unlawful for persons to apply for employment without federal work authorization. Moreover, it ruled that cases based upon allegations of racial profiling proceed through the courts, if such cases subsequently arise from stopping, detaining, or arresting undocumented persons. To this extent, the SCOTUS acted to ensure that the undocumented in Arizona *should retain their formal access* to federal protections against employment discrimination, notwithstanding the vigorous activism of citizens, at state and local levels, aimed at overriding such non-discrimination rights. It likewise *defended judicial rights of contestation* for undocumented immigrants, when the latter explicitly allege discrimination.

But, that said, the SCOTUS also upheld perhaps the most vital portion SB 1070, allowing Arizona state police to investigate the immigration status of those stopped, detained, or arrested, on a purportedly non-discriminatory 'reasonable suspicion' of not carrying immigration documents. Here, the majority opinion specified that state police not detain anyone on that ground for a prolonged amount of time. Nevertheless, this still allowed the Arizona state police considerable leeway to continue with the attrition policy of discriminatory targeting, inducing fear and terror of ongoing harassment among the undocumented to motivate them to deport themselves. Moreover, SB 1070 is by no means the only example of attempts to assert local – state and municipal – control over immigration in the US by following an attrition strategy. Indeed, it inspired a spate of related bills (which have proven unsuccessful to date) that would eliminate birthright citizenship unless both parents are US citizens, require proof of citizenship for all pupils registering in public schools or private schools. Some bills would even require hospitals to check immigration status before proceeding to care for patients (Ibid; for recent discussion of the undocumented and health care access, see Kuczewski 2016, as well as Berlinger and Rajeev 2013).

Overall, then, the significance of SB 1070 is that it vividly demonstrates the continued vulnerability of undocumented migrants to domination and internal persecution, despite the SCOTUS reaffirming against the state of Arizona, key non-discrimination and judicial contestation rights. I want to argue next, however, for a different approach to addressing such ongoing vulnerability. This does not consist in the intervention of judicial elites, such as Supreme Court Justices overruling domestic law and policy, when it contradicts decency. To be sure, this kind of top-down intervention is an important element of decency and non-domination. But it does not satisfactorily address the *unsettled and insecure status of the rights* of undocumented migrants arising from the bottom-up activism of citizens. Indeed, addressing this problem of insecurity entails assigning a participatory 'voice' to the undocumented in domestic processes of criticizing, discussing, debating, or altering their urgent rights, as persons with no legal right to be in the country. This establishes an *alternative form of bottom up activism* consisting in the exercise by undocumented migrants of an urgent human right to be political participant, wherever they are and wherever they are from.

4.4 The Urgent Human Right to Be a Political Participant, Wherever One Is

My argument so far has been (1) that there is a human right presumption against the state and in favor of undocumented migrants and (2) that, as interdependent with human rights, political participation by the undocumented is indispensable to the settlement of those urgent rights to which they are properly entitled, as a matter of decency. On the basis of (1) and (2), I have claimed (3) that decent peoples should embrace political participation as an urgent human right of global undocumented migrants. Nonetheless, this claim encounters an immediate objection to the effect that there is a much simpler solution to the problems of domination and internal persecution. Decent peoples could extend *rights of democratic citizenship* to the undocumented. This removes any need to add political participation to the list of urgent human rights recognized under the *Law of Peoples*. To be sure, the *Law of Peoples* does not presently recognize democratic citizenship as an urgent right, any more than it recognizes political participation by the undocumented as such a right in any decent society. After all, insisting upon democratic citizenship as human right would violate the commitment of the Law of Peoples to respect for non-democratic forms of society (Rawls 2001).

But, that said, creating a 'path to citizenship' for the undocumented does have some obvious practical and conceptual advantages, assuming the context of a minimally-democratic society. Here, there is a substantial literature on membership of such a society as a human right (see, for example, Christiano 2013; Buchanan 2007; Benhabib 2011). On the one hand, an obvious practical advantage is that a path to citizenship cleanly resolves the problems of de facto domination and internal persecution. It does so by establishing a *strict symmetry* of rights and opportunities for political participation, if the undocumented indeed become co-equal democratic citizens. If for no other reason, this follows to the extent that citizens cannot be deported, and so domination and persecution based upon the fear of retaliatory reporting to immigration authorities is out of the question. On the other hand, co-equal citizenship has the conceptual advantage of embracing the interdependency-relationship between participation and human rights: making democratic citizenship a human right ensures that all placed under coercion are better able to realize their other rights. There is thus no need to posit an interdependency relationship between human rights and political participation by the undocumented, expanding the scope of democratic citizenship to everyone within the territorial borders of the state. Moreover, expanding the scope of citizenship is surely preferable to a human right of political participation *sans* citizenship insofar as it avoids the perceptions of an assault on sovereignty and the exclusive rights of citizenship, as motivating nativist legislation like SB 1070.

Nonetheless, there is an obvious problem with such an expansion in the scope of democratic citizenship, in spite of its practical and conceptual advantages. Many undocumented indeed prize citizenship. Nevertheless, there is also plenty of evidence that it is not prized universally. This became evident from the resistance to SB 1070 by undocumented migrants, rising to the level of what I previously described as Gandhian moral heroism. SB 1070 led to a Repeal Coalition, involving many undocumented, which mobilized around the slogan 'to live, love and work anywhere you please' (Fernandez and Olsen 2011). Rather than demanding citizenship of the US, morally heroic undocumented participants in the coalition took the view that citizenship "should be no obstacle to participation in politics" (p. 416). Indeed, they became active political participants, without the benefit of citizenship, by demonstrating at city council meetings and conducting interviews with mass media outlets, such as radio, TV and newspapers. In these respects, their behavior as undocumented civil disobedients clearly departs from that of everyday resistance, eschewing explicit public appeals to principles of justice. It also departs from that of undocumented and unafraid, at least where the latter aligns with the Dreamer movement and the aspiration for citizenship. Instead, the political activism associated with the Repeal Coalition became one of explicit public address, often through legal and mainstream channels of public communication.

To this extent, undocumented participants in the Coalition engage in open public communication with the intention of shaping public opinion and *discursively* contributing (see, Dryzek 2006) to the formulation of a general legislative will. In this respect, their participation goes beyond the distinction I discussed in Chap. 2 between public communication and deliberation (Lefkowitz 2007). As activists in domestic political processes, the undocumented do not simply communicate their grievances to officialdom. In other words, they did not rely on justice-based pleas to elite officials – such as the SCOTUS Justices – for judicial intervention to protect their urgent human rights. Instead, they sought to participate in *shaping and influencing* the legislative will of citizens by contributing to deliberation and reason giving over the contents of law and policy. But such discursive participation does not otherwise entail contributing to sovereign-legislative decision outcomes *by casting votes*. Neither does it entail sharing in the collective responsibility for these decisions made *in the name of the people*. That, after all, would entail participation in universal suffrage and citizenship, which is *not* the Coalition demand. But, to this extent, discursive participation by undocumented migrants is not any kind of *assault* on democratic sovereignty, understood in the minimalist sense. At the most, activism and discursive political participation by the undocumented places on citizens a demand to justify publicly, in terms of decency and non-domination, *decisions* over which they ultimately retain sovereign control.

Nevertheless, if it can be rendered compatible with democratic minimalism, then a human right of undocumented migrants to be participants in domestic politics is not especially well captured by the slogan of the Repeal Coalition 'to live, love, and work anywhere you please.' Indeed, this slogan sounds like a libertarian demand for *free mobility* across international borders. In other words, it sounds like a demand for persons anywhere in the world to freely enter into contractual employment relations with whoever they please, or consensual intimate relations, without any regard to borders and citizenship (see, or example Carens 2015 and Kukathas 2013). But such a negative plea for *freedom from interference* with individual economic and associational liberties is not an especially good fit for what is actually a demand for a *positive right* of non-citizen *to freely* engage in the national battleground of politics. Rather than withdrawal by the state from interfering with associational relations between citizens and non-citizens, such a positive freedom to engage in this battleground requires that the state *should interfere* by taking active measures to ensure that these relations are non-dominating and non-persecutorial.

To be sure, a positive right of the undocumented to be political participants also entails its own imperative for free international mobility. After all, a consequence of globalization is the emergence of entirely new public spheres, based on multiple overlapping identities and political engagements, in different localities and territorial jurisdictions (Fernandez and Olsen 2011). Such new public spheres are inevitably "unstable" and changing by virtue of the constant "influx and outflow of persons" (Ibid). But they should nonetheless become the sites of domestic politics in which globally mobile persons may engage with sovereign citizens in order to work out decent terms of interaction. This requires that all decent societies acknowledge a binding obligation of justice to create an appropriate *institutional structure* in which the latter may exercise their human right to be political participants, without fear of intimidation and retaliation. Consequently, I turn next to the possibilities for providing national institutional arrangements, giving recognition and protection to such a novel human right.

4.5 Institutionally Embedding the Right to Be a Political Participant, Wherever One Is

My primary claim now is that the very different basic social and political structures of both democratic and hierarchical societies are compatible with a human right to be a political participant, wherever one is. Indeed, this is a conceptual possibility left open by my analysis from the previous section using the example of SB 1070. There, I argued that the undocumented might exercise their urgent human right to be active participants in domestic political processes, *without infringing upon* the basic arrangements of democratic minimalism. They may exercise this right without infringing upon these arrangements to the extent that the collective body of citizens, or people, retain sovereign control over and ultimate responsibility for how state coercive-power is exercised *in its name*. But, that said, it should also be possible to make a similar claim regarding the arrangements of a hierarchical society. That is, undocumented migrants in the latter category of society should also be able to exercise the same urgent human right to be participants, in its domestic political processes, without infringing upon its very different structure and arrangements. At any rate, this follows as long as the people of the hierarchical society retain its sovereign control over and ultimate responsibility for how state coercive-power is exercised in its name.

Moreover, a human right of undocumented migrants to be participants in domestic political processes is *no less urgent* in a hierarchical society than in a democratic society. After all, an asymmetry of power between citizens and non-citizens also characterizes hierarchical societies. This, of course, is not manifest in terms of a difference between those who can and cannot exercise equal rights of participation and suffrage and voting. Instead, it is manifest in terms of a difference between those whom the hierarchical people do and not recognize as belonging to any one or other of its stratified social groups. Here, the issue between citizens and undocumented is not, strictly speaking, *inequality* of rights. It is not this because, in a consultation hierarchy, rights are distributed differentially, anyway, based on group memberships. To this extent, citizens do not enjoy equality of political and civil rights as characteristic of democracies. The power asymmetry between citizens and undocumented, then, consists in the latter's effective exclusion from the hierarchy of consultation in which the different needs and interests of various social groups are represented to the society's ruling elites. But this phenomenon of an entrenched power asymmetry based on exclusion from the system of institutions designed to represent the needs and interests of all those subject to the state's coercive power is remarkably similar to the power asymmetry between citizens and undocumented in democracies.

It is remarkably similar in the sense that this asymmetry is also one of effective exclusion from the system of basic institutions in which rights are distributed. But, as my previous analyses show, undocumented migrants are still effectively excluded from claiming those rights distributed to them within the basic institutional structure of democracies. My point, then, is that both categories of society create power asymmetries between citizens and undocumented. They do so to the extent neither has created institutions that might allow the latter to be effective in claiming these rights, as domestic political participants. What, though, is the most plausible form of institutional arrangements that might be applicable *to any decent society* for the recognition and protections of a human right to be a political participant, wherever one is? I want to argue that the kind of institutional arrangements characteristic of Rawls' concept of the traditional-hierarchical society provide a suitable model for embedding such an urgent positive right of participation.

At any rate, these non-democratic arrangements provide a good model in a way that a *democratic interpretation* of an urgent human right of undocumented migrants to be political participants clearly do not. Indeed, if a human right to be a participant in domestic politics is read as a human right to be a citizen of a democratic state, then it fails to capture the kind of imperative identified by many undocumented migrants for participation in the public spheres of more than just one country (Fernandez and Olsen 2011). Hence, besides its inappropriateness for peoples committed to non-democratic arrangements, the model of democratic citizenship fails as candidate for a human right of persons committed to ongoing cross-border mobility. Of course, a human right to be a citizen of any decent society, and not just a democratic society, would likewise fail to capture this mobility imperative. Clearly, a right to stay and to become a citizen of a hierarchical society, fitting somewhere into its existing strata of social groups, fares no better in this respect. So, what exactly is promising about the arrangements of hierarchical societies for an urgent human right to be a political participant, wherever one is?

This promise lies precisely in the conception of a *differential order of rights*. Here, some nuancing of the claim concerning such an urgent human right to be political participants in decent societies is required. On the one hand, such a human right applies equally to all persons everywhere, in the same way as urgent human rights to non-subordination and subsistence. But, on the other hand, just as urgent rights to non-servitude and subsistence may be fitted into a much larger hierarchical order of differentially distributed rights, the same can be said about an urgent right of undocumented migrants to be participants in the domestic politics of any decent society they might enter. To this extent, a human right of this sort would be *both* equally distributed *and* fitted into a hierarchy of citizens and undocumented, where the former might enjoy equal political and civil rights or differentially distributed rights, depending on whether it is democratically or hierarchically ordered. Indeed, even if they may also enjoy equal non-discrimination rights in a democratic society, the undocumented are still in a *hierarchical relationship with citizens*, bearing the exclusive rights and collective responsibility of sovereignty.

Consequently, decency and non-domination require the provision of an appropriate *consultation procedure* for undocumented migrants as possessing a differential set of rights from citizens: that is, rights of contestation and dissent detached from the rights and responsibilities of sovereignty unique to the collective body of citizens or people. Such a consultation procedure entails recognizing that everyone placed under coercion by the state has an urgent right to discursively participate in shaping the terms of such coercion. Here, discursive participation by the undocumented are channeled through some formal procedure of consultation with citizens, as indeed collectively responsible for deciding and enforcing law and policy. In this respect, a condition of legitimacy for law and policy – over which citizens ultimately retain sovereign control – would be that all relevantly affected groups are consulted, their voices represented, and their contestations given uptake and answered on the basis of publicly defensible reasons appealing to decency. Consistent with my remarks from the previous chapter regarding a firewall (Carens 2015) between participation and law enforcement, any formal consultation procedures representing the undocumented to the people should be held separate from enforcement so that deportation proceedings may not be initiated based on these procedures.

But, more importantly, a consultation protocol giving a participatory voice to the undocumented is consistent with Rawls' conception of a hierarchy of social groups with very different *needs and interests*. Indeed, the consultation procedure does not assume that the needs and interests of citizens and undocumented are necessarily fungible or interchangeable (Guinier 1995), when they are not. Not only do some undocumented have interests in becoming citizens, as interests they do not share with those who are already citizens, but also other undocumented have interests in ongoing cross-border mobility, as interests that are, again, not shared with citizens settled within their own national borders. Obviously, then, the undocumented must be represented, in a formal consultation procedure, based on how their needs and interests are fundamentally different from those of citizens. But this leaves open the question of *who* should represent the different needs and interests of the undocumented, in such formal procedures. Should citizens represent the undocumented or should the undocumented represent the undocumented? Given that the interests of citizens and undocumented are not fungible, the latter possibility might seem by far preferable. This might seem so on the reasonable assumption that citizens representing the undocumented are *less likely* to remain true to the fundamental interests of the latter in becoming citizens or in securing the condition of non-domination, while continuing to move back and forth across borders (Fernandez and Olsen 2011).

That said, however, there is perhaps no compelling reason to deny that citizens can also represent the undocumented in formal consultation procedures. Indeed, citizens may represent the undocumented on the fiduciary model of a trustee/beneficiary relationship (Thomsen 2013). Here, the trustee's interests may never perfectly mirror those of the undocumented. Nonetheless, the possibility for conflict to arise between the non-fungible interests of trustees and beneficiaries may be reduced, if the latter choose the former or, at the very least, have input into the appointment of citizen trustees (perhaps exercising a veto power over the appointment of 'trustees' they do not trust). Insisting that concrete penalties may be imposed by the undocumented-beneficiaries, such as the removal of citizen-trustees from their position should they violate trust, further reduces the potential for conflict. These practical safeguards against conflicts of interests may just as well apply to undocumented-trustees. Even though the fundamental interests of undocumented may be fungible or interchangeable, there is always a potential for undocumented-trustees to become susceptible to corruption when holding a position of relative power in the consultation hierarchy.

Crucially, however, it should *not* be supposed that the "primary goal of … trustees should be the realization of full actual representation for the undocumented" (Ibid, p. 29). At any rate, this should not be the goal if 'full actual representation' means "actual involvement in the process of determining the process of *membership acquisition*" (Ibid). Indeed, membership acquisition – becoming a citizen, a *member of the people* – may be *a* goal of fiduciary representation by trustees. That is, determining a path to citizenship for the undocumented may be *one of the goals* of such representation with respect to those undocumented who desire citizenship. But it is not the primary or overarching goal of fiduciary representation for the undocumented, insofar as this may involve also representing an interest in continued cross-border mobility, without also claiming the status of citizen and membership of the people. In other words, such representation does not depend on membership acquisition at all. Instead, it permits some wide variability with respect to how undocumented migrants may conceive their interests differently, in response to the pressures of globalization. Indeed, the goals of fiduciary representation may be plural, whether the trustees are citizens or undocumented. Moreover, these goals remain plural whether the consultation procedures for representing the undocumented are those belonging to democratic or hierarchical societies.

I have argued, then, that the model of fiduciary or trustee representation of those who do not participate in sovereign decision-making or partake in collective responsibility for sovereign-legislative decisions best characterizes an appropriate institutional response to the plight of the undocumented. This corrects for the inadequacy of elite judicial rulings in countering the activism of nativist citizens when this runs counter to decency, as in my earlier case of SB 1070 in the US. Indeed, I assume here that the problem of nativist citizen activism may be just as acute in hierarchical as democratic societies. After all, the same kind of power asymmetry would exists between the citizens of hierarchical societies and undocumented migrants living, loving, and working within their borders. Stratified according to distinct social groups with differential rights and duties, the citizens of such societies may not have the same range of opportunities for political activism as the free and equal citizens of democracies. But the hierarchical procedures of consultation for such diverse groups themselves may become channels for the expression of nativist sentiment and resentment towards outsiders, thus placing considerable pressure on elite rulers to compromise the people's commitment to decency. In this respect, appropriate participation by the undocumented is no less important in terms of establishing an alternative mode of discourse and contestation placing binding human rights claims on elites and people alike.

That said, I want next to explore further the idea of trustee representation by way of adapting the idea of deliberative mini-publics. At first, this might seem surprising. After all, mini-publics are typically understood as innovations specifically within democratic theory (Boker and Estlub 2015). Nonetheless, I argue that there is an *implicitly hierarchical component* to mini-publics that allows for the possibility of their adaptation to hierarchical societies. Moreover, allowing for such adaptation to hierarchical as well as democratic societies, I argue that mini-publics are especially well suited to address the idea of trustee representation applied to the undocumented migrants. In particular, I argue that they present a way to prioritize the idea of undocumented discursively representing undocumented within the institutional frameworks of both categories of society. Indeed, inherently hierarchical mini-publics elide problems otherwise arising for the fiduciary model of trustee representation. As I discuss next, these are problems concerning the selection and removal of trustees and the permanent or transitory nature of fora for representing persons who have no legal right to be in the country and might not even want to stay for any prolonged length of time.

4.6 A Proposal for Transitory Hierarchical Mini-Publics

Understood in light of democratic theory, the standard idea of a mini-public is that it is composed of a representative sample of *randomly selected* citizens. Indeed, mini-publics bring together randomly selected *citizens*, often on the model of a deliberative jury, to deliver a verdict on the merits of particular law and policy proposals before the people. In this respect, they call citizens to deliberate a public controversy concerning both the efficacy and legitimacy of proposed legislation. Rarely, however, is their verdict conceived in terms of binding law. Instead, it is sometimes conceived it purely discursive terms. Here, the goal is for it to be circulated through the various channels of mass public communication and deliberation so that the verdict can then be deliberated by the larger mass democratic public. It this way, it contributes to the discursive process of shaping and influencing the formulation of the general legislative will (Dryzek 2006). But a mini-public verdict may also be conceived as placing binding obligations on officials of the state to give uptake and consideration. Officials are thus not bound to produce legislation mirroring the mini-public verdict. Nonetheless, they are bound to respond to the verdict by giving publicly accessible reasons for accepting or rejecting it, whether in whole or in part. Consequently, officials do not just give their reasons to the mini-public participants, but also to the people as a whole so that they may likewise be circulated through the channels of mass communication. In this respect, the public reasons of officials, again, discursively contribute to shaping the people's collective legislative will.

But, despite these deep ties to democracy, my claim is that mini-publics may be seen as aligned with the idea of a consultation hierarchy. Indeed, solicitation by the state of a deliberative jury verdict is a mode of *consultation* with a representative sample of those who are potentially affected by legislation and its coercive enforcement. But uptake for the verdict (by the mass democratic public or officials of the state or both) is also *hierarchical*. At any rate, it is hierarchical at least in the sense that the randomly selected participants in the mini-public must ultimately *defer* to the legislative will of the sovereign people. Of course, such deference by the randomly selected citizens of the mini-public is a merely temporary feature of consultation preliminary to inclusive democratic processes of representing the whole people through suffrage and voting by all citizens, as free and equal. To this extent, decision-making and responsibility-taking following consultation includes those participants in the mini-public who delivered their verdict for mass public consumption and consideration.

But still there is clearly a *hierarchy of authority* between, on the one hand, consultants and, on the other hand, decision-makers and responsibility-takers. This hierarchy of authority between consultation and decision-making is important to my present discussion insofar as it opens up the possibility of mini-publics that *remain hierarchical* in the sense their participants defer to the sovereign authority of a ruling elite. Here, consultants defer not to the collective body of free and equal citizens as in a democracy, but instead to an elite exercising sovereign decision-making power. Although not popularly elected, such an elite remains duty-bound to publicly explain and justify its decisions and uses of coercion to the hierarchical people, according to the human rights standards of decency. But, if this is so, then there is no insurmountable conceptual obstacle to adapting the mini-public concept to a hierarchical society. A mini-public could be convened within the framework of a hierarchical society that defers to an elite, which is answerable to the people in light of human rights standards, but not elected on the basis of universal suffrage.

Indeed, when applied to the undocumented, mini-publics would have an unavoidably hierarchical character in a democratic society as well. A mini-public of the undocumented in a democracy would ultimately defer to the politically egalitarian structure of decision making among free and equal citizens as authoritative. But the hierarchy of consultation and decision-making between undocumented and sovereign democratic citizens would remain fixed. At any rate, it would remain fixed to the extent that undocumented participants in the mini-public would not also be participants in any subsequent processes of suffrage and voting on a basis of equality with citizens. If consultation with a mini-public of undocumented resulted in a decision to create a path to citizenship, then the latter would be a sovereign democratic decision authorized by citizens. Consequently, hierarchical consultation without participation in sovereign decision-making would be a characteristic of mini-public participation by the undocumented in both categories of society.

In addition to being adaptable to both democratic and hierarchical societies, the concept of the mini-public resolves some practical problems arising from the fiduciary model of trustee representation floated earlier. For example, how are the undocumented to select trustee-representatives when they have no documented status in the country? Moreover, how are they to remove trustees from their positions? It is unclear what mechanisms the state could establish to ensure that selection and removal processes for representatives are free from manipulation and corruption. Nevertheless, problem is not insoluble. The undocumented might be issued a transnational identity card by the state (Ansley 2010), which could be used to register at polling booths monitored by an independent agency. This would entail suffrage for the undocumented in selecting trustee-representatives, if not universal suffrage in the popular democratic processes of representative decision and responsibility taking that remain exclusive to citizens. To be sure, this approach might be a more awkward fit for hierarchical societies. After all, it attributes to the undocumented a kind of moral equality, in selecting representatives, denied to citizens. But, as amounting to 'suffrage without sovereignty' for the undocumented, it does not otherwise pose a direct challenge to the hierarchical order of non-electoral representation and decision-making, any more than it poses such a threat to the universal suffrage of citizens in a democracy.

That said, however, the random selection of undocumented trustee participants would still encounter similar problems in both categories of society: viz. how does the state randomly select a representative sample of persons without documentation? This concern may be addressed, however, through a transnational identity register, again administered by an independent agency. Nevertheless, it could also be addressed by backing down somewhat from the earlier claim regarding the fiduciary-representation model that trustees for the undocumented should not be volunteers (Thomsen 2013). Hence, a hierarchical mini-public might draw from a population of those undocumented who are willing to submit their names for a lottery for the random-selection of representative trustee-participants. Volunteering for this pool of potential participants would be accompanied by immunity to deportation (Carens 2015). Undoubtedly, such a model of random selection from a pool of undocumented volunteers will entail an element of self-selection by comparison with, say, randomly selecting citizens from the voter rolls (although here it is perhaps also worth pointing out that citizens 'volunteer' to register as voters). Nevertheless, randomly selecting from a volunteer pool of undocumented is still a far cry from self-appointment or government appointment. It ensures some considerable independence of trustee-participants, none of whom may simply 'grab' the position of trustee to advance a narrow agenda. Moreover, immunity to deportation should guarantee that the pool is large enough to permit the representation of plural undocumented points of view by means of random selection.

Indeed, a further possible advantage to the model of the hierarchical mini-public is that it resolves the problem of how to remove trustees who abuse their position. Indeed, mini-publics elide this problem to the extent they are always transitory fora. Trustee participants address specific issues on the legislative agenda importantly affecting (Gould 2013). But the fora are subsequently dissolved, once the participants have concluded their deliberations and issued their verdict. Consequently, corrupt and unrepresentative trustee- participants do not have to be pried out of positions they wish to make permanent. Nevertheless, an important difference remains concerning the verdict of hierarchical mini-publics, comprised of undocumented trustee-participants, in democratic and hierarchical societies, respectively.

As previously noted, there is, strictly speaking, no *mass* public of free and equal citizens in Rawls' concept of a hierarchical society (2001). Instead, there are multiple stratified social groups – or rather multiple domestic publics – defined by their differential rights and duties within the non-democratic order. This inevitably raises a question as to the proper *addressees* of the mini-public verdict in a hierarchical society, if not a mass democratic public ultimately taking collective responsibility through universal suffrage and voting for legislative outcomes given in its name? The answer, of course, is that it is the ruling elite of the hierarchical society. That is, the elite not only responsible for ensuring its rulings are consistent with the differential rights of citizens and the urgent rights of everyone within the territorial borders of the state, but also publicly explaining these rulings to all affected parties, citizen and undocumented.

This elite is thus the *direct* addressee of the verdict of undocumented trustee-participants in a hierarchical mini-public. But the multiple publics of citizens possessing differential rights and statuses who collectively make up the hierarchical people are also *indirectly* addressees of the verdict. They are indirectly addressees in the sense that the ruling elite must explain its judgments regarding what is owed to undocumented migrants to such diverse groups of citizens, whose needs and interests are neither fungible with those of the undocumented nor, for that matter, with one another. To this extent, the elites circulate the mini-public verdict throughout the multiple and diverse social groups characterizing the hierarchical society. In this respect, they stimulating a generalized process of public reconsideration based on their common good conception of justice, without reference to the idea of democratic and a mass public of free and equal citizens.

4.7 Conclusion

My purpose in this chapter was to build upon the argument of the previous chapter concerning the moral right of undocumented migrants to disobey. Indeed, I have argued in this chapter for a human right of the undocumented to be political participants in domestic politics. Political participation is coextensive with realizing the urgent rights of non-domination and non-persecution to which all migrant persons are properly entitled within the territorial borders of a decent society, regardless of whether they actually have a legal right to be there. Such a human right to be a political participant is not a legal right to stay, or a right not to be deported. Instead, it is a right to have a participatory voice in shaping and influencing the sovereign decisions of citizens when these importantly affect the needs and interests of the undocumented. As a human right, participation by the undocumented in domestic politics is compatible with democracy, but it is also compatible with Rawls's concept of a decent hierarchical society. In this latter respect, I have argued for both categories of society may embed such a right in their institutional arrangements, proposing the model of hierarchical mini-publics.

Primarily, though, the argument of this chapter builds on the argument of the previous one in the sense that a human right of the undocumented to be domestic political participants is the most appropriate legal reform in response to undocumented disobedience. It is more appropriate not only insofar as it avoids the false assumption that all undocumented want to stay, but also in that it preserves the right of peoples to make immigration decisions and control their territorial borders. That is, it preserves this sovereign right of both democratic and hierarchical peoples, on the presumption they exercise this right consistently with human rights. As coextensive with other urgent rights including non-domination and non-persecution, a human right of the undocumented to be political participants in domestic politics enables decent peoples to meet this presumption. Indeed, having satisfied an urgent right to the undocumented to be such participants, any further gains realized by the undocumented migrants will be a function of their discursive participation in shaping and influencing the sovereign decisions of decent peoples, democratic or hierarchical.

References

Abizadeh, Arash. 2008. Democratic Theory and Border Coercion: No Right to Unilaterally Control Your Own Borders. *Political Theory* 36(1): 37–65.

Ansley, Fran. 2010. *Constructing Citizenship Without a License. Studies in Social Justice* 4(2): 165–170.

Arat, Zehra. 2006. Forging a Global Human Rights Culture: Origins and Prospects of the International Bill of Rights. *Human Rights Quarterly* 28(2): 416–437.

Benhabib, Seyla. 2011. Is There a Human Right to Democracy? Beyond Interventionism and Indifference. In *Dignity in Adversity: Human Rights in Troubled Times*. Cambridge: Polity Press.

Benton, Meghan. 2010. The Tyranny of the Enfranchised Majority? The Accountability of States to their Non-Citizen Population. *Res Publica* 16: 397–413.

Berlinger, Nancy, and Ragharan Rajeev. 2013. *The Ethics of Advocacy for Undocumented Patients. Hastings Center Report* 43(1): 14–17.

Boker, Marit, and Stephen Estlub. 2015. The Possibility of Critical Deliberative Mini Publics: Realpolitik and the Normative Cycles of Democratic Theory. *Representation* 51(2): 125–144.

Buchanan, Allen. 2007. *Justice, Legitimacy and Self-Determination*. Oxford: Oxford University Press.

Carens, Joseph. 2015. *The Ethics of Immigration*. Oxford: Oxford University Press.

Christiano, Thomas. 2013. An Egalitarian Argument for a Human Right to Democracy. In *Human Rights: The Hard Cases*, ed. Cindy Holder and David Reidy, 301–326. Cambridge: Cambridge University Press.

Dryzek, John. 2006. *Deliberative Global Politics*. Cambridge: Polity Press.

Fernandez, Luis, and Joel Olsen. 2011. *To Live Love and Work Anywhere You Please. Contemporary Political Philosophy* 10: 412–418.

Gould, Carol. 2013. The Human Right to Democracy and its Global Import. In *Human Rights: The Hard Cases*, ed. Cindy Holder and David Reidy, 285–3000. Cambridge: Cambridge University Press.

Guinier, Lani. 1995. *Tyranny of the Majority: Fundamental Fairness in Representative Democracy*. New York: Free Press.

Kuczewski, Mark. 2016. *The Really New Jim Crow: Why Bioethicists Must Ally with Undocumented Migrants. American Journal of Bioethics* 16(4): 21–23.
Kukathas, Chandran. 2013. *The Liberal Archipelago: A Theory of Diversity and Freedom*. Oxford: Oxford University Press.
Lefkowitz, David. 2007. On a Moral Right to Civil Disobedience. *Ethics* 117(2): 202–233.
Nicholls, Walter. 2013. Making Undocumented Immigrants into a Legitimate Political Subject: Theoretical Observations from the United States and France. *Theory, Culture, and Society* 30(3): 82–107.
Rawls, John. 2001. *The Law of Peoples*. Cambridge, MA: Harvard University Press.
Reidy, David. 2012. On the Human Right to Democracy: Searching for Sense Without Stilts. *Journal of Social Philosophy* 43(2): 177–203.
Riker, Walter. 2014. Human Rights Without Political Participation? *Human Rights Review* 15: 369–390.
Sen, Amartya. 2000. *Development as Freedom*. New York: Doubleday Anchor.
Shue, Henry. 1996. *Basic Rights: Subsistence, Affluence, and US Foreign Policy*. Princeton: Princeton University Press.
Thomsen, Kyle. 2013. Crossing the Divide: Marginalized Populations and the Dilemma of Deliberative Democracy. In *Civic Virtue, Divided Societies, and Democratic Dilemmas*, 21–35. Charlottesville: Philosophy Documentation Centre.
Walzer, Michael. 1984. *Spheres of Justice: A Defense of Pluralism and Equality*. New York: Basic Books.
Wellman, Christopher, and Philip Cole. 2011. *Debating the Ethics of Immigration: Is There a Right to Exclude?* Oxford: Oxford University Press.

Chapter 5
Unfair Terms of Global Cooperation and the Fair Equality of Liberty Between Peoples

Abstract In this chapter, I turn from undocumented populations to the global poor, as subjects of representative claim making by more affluent disobedient actors from both liberal and hierarchical societies. Indeed, I develop the idea of civil disobedience as representative claim making by such actors to compensate for the inability of the poorest and most desperate inhabitants of the planet to exercise any influence over the multiple structures and agencies of global governance. These structures and agencies range from different types of nation states to International Governmental Organizations (IGOs), International Financial Organizations (IFOs), International Non-Governmental Organizations (INGOs), and so on. Here, a global perspective represents concern for the poorest, the sickest, and the hungriest at different sites and locations of global rule making. Such a perspective combines multinational coalitions of cosmopolitan citizens challenging the rulings and decisions of this or that IGO or IFO with states challenging the structure of international law as differentially impacting rich and poor. The approach I take in this chapter offers a third way between duties of assistance to the poor and global distributive justice. It does so by highlighting instead the normative equality assigned to peoples in *Law of Peoples* (2001). It does so by justifying disobedience by cosmopolitan citizens and states as contesting the *unfair value of liberty* between peoples in international rule making. In this respect, my approach offers a significant reinterpretation of the duty of assistance. It reinterprets the duty as prescribing assistance or help in the creation of a well-ordered international community of peoples, based on the fair value of their liberty in international agreements on trade and economic justice. However, it does not rule out progress towards egalitarian global distributive justice. My primary concern is with justifying disobedience by cosmopolitan citizens and states in the circumstance of piecewise global justice in which the value of liberty for peoples is unfair. It does not take a stand on particular schemes or policies of distributive justice, regarding these important policy matters as separate from the justification for resorting to civil disobedience.

M. Allen, *Civil Disobedience in Global Perspective*,
Studies in Global Justice 16, DOI 10.1007/978-94-024-1164-5_5

5.1 Introduction

My discussion of undocumented disobedients was intended to show that they are civil disobedients proper capable of placing peoples under binding obligations of uptake and reconsideration. It established an urgent human right of the undocumented to be political participants, wherever they are. This took the discussion of civil disobedience in global perspective from intra-state disobedience relations between co-nationals to such intra-state relations between non-nationals and co-nationals. In this chapter, I expand the discussion in two ways. On the one hand, I consider intra-state disobedience relations between cosmopolitan citizens and the global community of peoples, including the pluralism of new structures of global governance it has generated under globalization. To be sure, undocumented disobedients are cosmopolitan citizens to the extent they exercise an urgent human right to be political participants. But they do so specifically in the context of the domestic politics of the society whose borders they have crossed and in which they are vulnerable to interpersonal domination. By contrast, I use 'cosmopolitan citizens' to refer to diverse kinds of moral agents protesting the terms of cooperation for the global governance system. To this extent, cosmopolitan citizens do not necessarily protest the terms of domestic politics in any particular decent society. Here, the scope of their disobedience public address is international rather than national and their addressee is the international community of peoples rather than this or that national people. On the other hand, I consider inter-state disobedience relations between peoples challenging the complex and multiple structures of global governance: that is, structures owing their existence to the delegated authority of peoples, beholden to protecting urgent human rights. As collective moral agents, peoples are also cosmopolitan citizens, sharing the profound concerns of other such citizens with the piecewise just character of the global system.

Indeed, both new cases of disobedience in a global perspective discussed in this chapter respond to the piecewise character of global economic justice. Globalization has brought all peoples under international terms of economic cooperation. Nevertheless, in too many instances, these terms are profoundly unfair or unjust, especially to the poorest and most vulnerable inhabitants of the planet. In *Law of Peoples* (2001), Rawls argues that rich peoples owe to poor peoples duties of assistance. These duties, however, do not demand that the transferal of resources from rich to more peoples. More often than not, poor peoples of so-called burdened societies are poor because of their historical, social, and economic circumstances (2001). Laboring under these circumstances, such societies are in state of dis-order from the standpoint of justice. To this extent, rich peoples owe them assistance, or help, to become well ordered. This help consists mostly in giving them advice grounded in human rights considerations, as opposed to regulating global economic inequalities. Consequently, the duty of assistance advances an idea of orderliness (Loriaux 2012), rather than resource distribution. Here, orderliness does not necessarily entail liberal egalitarian justice. Instead, it could entail a common good conception of justice, without an egalitarian distribution of civil and political rights, or a principle of distributive economic justice, along the lines of Rawls' difference principle is his earlier *Theory of Justice* (1971).

This prescribes that economic differences should be justified as bringing benefits to the worst off participants in domestic cooperation, unavailable to them under an alternative distributive scheme. Specific to domestic justice for liberal democracies, the difference principle is part of Rawls' (2001) strategy for creating a fair value of equal liberties for all citizens by giving them the opportunities and resources they need to pursue the kinds of lives they choose for themselves. For his part, however, Rawls did not extend the difference principle to the international political order. He did not do so for two reasons. On the one hand, he wanted to avoid imposing a liberal egalitarian conception of justice onto peoples subscribing to an alternative common good conception: that would contradict the liberal principle of toleration for non-liberal points of view. On the other hand and closely related to the first reason, he wanted to offer a conceptualization of an international community well ordered by justice that could accommodate both liberal and non-liberal points of view. This conceptualization entails appeal to the inclusive idea of decency and the reasonableness of peoples, with different moral characters.

In contrast to his stress on the duty of assistance, Rawls' critics develop the cosmopolitan implications of his theory of domestic distributive justice by advocating a global extension of the difference principle (Beitz 2008; Moellendorf 2008; Pogge 1989; for influential critiques of this position, see Blake 2001; Brock 2005; Miller 2005; for a defense of Rawls on global justice, see Reidy 2007). This extension prescribes that the richest countries of the world redistribute wealth and resources to the globally worst off, without regard to the morally arbitrary factors of birthplace and nationality. Others emphasize economic redistribution by rich countries to the global poor, according to some alternative mechanism, such as a global resource dividend (Pogge 2008). Stressing global economic redistribution over duties of assistance and advice, this version of cosmopolitanism thus attempts to resolve the problem of global poverty through resource transferals. As such, it need not be understood as an attempt by liberal-democratic peoples to impose their principles of domestic economic justice onto the rest of the world. It is simply an attempt to feed the hungry. Nevertheless, cosmopolitans often see resource transferals as much more than a concern with feeding the hungry that is neutral between competing conceptions of justice. Indeed, they intend such transferals as part of a larger scheme of liberal-democratic social justice writ large (Held 2004; Caney 2006). Here, the aim is to create a fair value of liberty for all persons in the world by giving to them resources and opportunities to lead the kinds of lives they would want and choose for themselves.

Here, poverty relief is not neutral between conceptions of justice, but a step along the way to creating more egalitarian opportunities in terms of global access to education, job markets, and so on (Cud 2013). In doing so, however, global resource redistributions run into precisely the problem Rawls sought to avoid by embracing duties of assistance: that is, a failure of toleration for alternative non-liberal conceptions of justice. Indeed, the ideal of toleration between peoples laid out by Rawls in *Law of Peoples* (2001) effectively restricts rich peoples to the duty of assistance. Nevertheless, this is not because of some callous disregard among rich peoples for the depredations of global poverty. Instead, toleration between peoples reflects a concern with showing respect for the autonomy of different peoples, when addressing difficult questions of poverty and economic development within the terms of their own cultural paradigms of justice. As I understand him, Rawls intends help and advice, as prescriptions of the duty of justice, to be expressions of respect for autonomy. To the extent they become well-ordered according the particular conception of justice expressing the moral character of their peoples, burdened societies are empowered to take appropriate steps to promote their own economic development, as they see fit. This is consistent with the normative priority (Risse 2015) of states and peoples, as collectively autonomous actors on the global state, and primary subjects of responsibility taking for human rights (Beitz 2011).

In this respect, I contend that the problem with Rawls' notion of duties of assistance is not that they aim to promote an ideal of orderliness (Loriaux 2012) rather than demanding resource transfers. Instead, the problem is the limitation of such duties to giving advice. My claim is that the duty to promote orderliness, throughout the international community of states and peoples, encompasses the moral right to civil disobedience. This is not to say that civilly disobedient protests by cosmopolitan citizens – or states acting as cosmopolitan citizens – is a *duty* as opposed to a right. It is only to say that civilly disobedient protests, contesting the piecewise character of global economic justice (Ogunye 2015), are one legitimate way to fulfill this duty, which Rawls himself failed to consider. Here, I take it that civil disobedience is an attempt to highlight some fundamental injustice and call for peoples, as collectively responsible moral agents, to reconsider present law and policy, rather than advocate for any particular policy agenda. It is thus a call for reconsideration and deliberation among peoples and their representatives, not a strategy calculated to advance a predetermined policy agenda. In what sense, though, does civil disobedience, as opposed to giving human rights advice, promote a more orderly international community of peoples, in which poverty relief and economic development is an expression of the autonomy of different peoples, with different moral characters?

The answer to this question is that it turns the focus of attention from burdened societies to those rich and powerful societies that presently dominate international rule-making. Indeed, disobedience by cosmopolitan citizens and states opens a global discourse on the fairness of the present rules of global economic cooperation. Here, rich and powerful societies are challenged to stop giving human rights advice and instead critically look at themselves and their role in perpetuating a disordered global system. This, however, is a system of global economic cooperation between peoples, and not persons. Consequently, the issue for disobedient cosmopolitan citizens and states is not the economic terms of cooperation for *persons* to realize the fair value of their liberty in pursuing their individual life-goals. Instead, the issue is the terms of cooperation for *peoples* to realize such a value in pursuing their collective goals for development in the global economy. The issue, in other words, is the *fair value of liberty between peoples* in the pursuit of national economic self-development. This fair value for peoples is a function of the reasonableness criterion, as applied to peoples and not persons under the Law of Peoples (Rawls 2001). Indeed, the value of liberty for peoples is *unfair* when only some but not all peoples are able to exercise their equal liberty, or autonomy, in shaping international processes of global rule-making. An unfair value of liberty between peoples means that the global system is disordered. Consequently, reasonable peoples ought to reconsider their share of responsibility for this piecewise condition of justice.

Civilly disobedient global public address, then, is a response to a condition of unfairness in which powerful forces for inequality retain their influence over global cooperation because they "never have to face the massed power of the globally dispossessed" (Walzer 1999, 209). After all, the multiplication and dispersal of authorities necessary for global governance – including IGOs, IFOs, and NGOs – preclude the formation of a singular global arena in which the poor, the sick, and the hungry of the world could speak with a single unified voice (Ibid). The approach I take, however, does not attempt to create a singular forum for the globally worst off, any more than it advocates for a particular resource redistribution scheme. Instead, it looks to disobedient cosmopolitan citizen and states to assist, or help, create a more orderly world by binding peoples to uptake and reconsideration, in light of such asymmetry relations of power and influence. This does not mean that the globally worst off – the poorest, sickest, and hungriest – should take on the role of disobedients (Ogunye 2015). It is undoubtedly the moral right of the globally dispossessed to resort to such disobedience. Nevertheless, the worst off in the global system of cooperation presently lack the resources necessary to mount sustained global disobedience campaigns, effectively gaining the attention of the global public. Consequently, responsibility for contesting the fairness of global cooperation properly falls to those more affluent actors possessing the resources as well as organizational skills for such campaigns. In other words, responsibility falls to cosmopolitan citizens of multinational coalitions of activists or different kinds of states – both liberal-democratic and traditional-hierarchical – representing their people's sincere and considered belief that the terms of international cooperation are unfair and exploitative.

In what sense, however, do such affluent and influential disobedients represent the global poor? It is perhaps tempting to say that they 'stand for' or 'act for' (Pitkin 1971) the global poor, thereby representing to a diverse global public those who lack the resources to speak for themselves. That, however, is a particularly difficult move to justify (for a more optimistic view of its justification, see Allen 2015). Certainly, the global poor do not elect coalitions of cosmopolitan citizens to act on their behalf. Moreover, states engaging in disobedient acts may represent the concern of their own people with global economic injustice. But, again, the notion that rich states should take it upon themselves to represent the citizens of burdened societies is obviously problematic. Nonetheless, I shall argue that disobedience by cosmopolitan citizens does serve a certain kind of representative function. This is not to represent the perspective of the globally worst off as much as represent the perspective of a concerned global public, in a double sense. On the one hand, it represents a perspective of global public concern about the depredations of global poverty. But, on the other hand, it represents a perspective of global public concern about the unfair value of liberty between peoples, whereby only some but not other peoples effectively contribute to global rule making.

I arrange this chapter in the following steps. First, I briefly return to Rawls' framework for civil disobedience in order to consider the representative function of the disobedient act, emphasizing that this function can be detached from the idea of electoral representation. I then discuss civil disobedience by cosmopolitan citizens as multinational coalitions as well as liberal-democratic and traditional-hierarchical states representing the perspective of a concerned global public about global poverty and the fair value of liberty among rich and poor peoples. Nevertheless, I also point to some difficulties with the notion of the citizens of traditional-hierarchical states performing the role of disobedients. Finally, I discuss the need for some further revision to the Rawlsian framework with respect to engaging rather than avoiding controversies over global distributive equity.

5.2 Civil Disobedience and Representation

In liberal-democratic societies, civil disobedience is a way of contesting the outcomes of electoral representation and democratic majoritarianism (Rawls 1971). Here, disobedients appeal to liberal principles of justice, such as equal liberty and fair equality of opportunity, as the standard for evaluating the legitimacy of democratic expressions the majority will and its representation by elected officials standing or acting for the people (Pitkin 1972). Thus slightly adapting Rawls' (1971) language of the invitation to reconsider, disobedients invite the majority of citizens to consider whether they believe their sovereign democratic will aligns with fundamental principles of liberal justice. Disobedients thus invite the majority to consider whether it has properly expressed its commitment to these principles through the key majoritarian institutions of voting and representation. Here, the disobedience itself is not a representative act, but instead a question posed to those who would claim that democratic majoritarianism is already an adequate expression of justice represented by the elected officials of the state. Nevertheless, I want to argue that it is also possible to reinterpret disobedient acts as particular kinds of representative acts. Obviously, any such reinterpretation will have to overcome the immediate objection that disobedience takes place outside the established parameters of voting and representation. To be sure, elected representatives of the people may be civil disobedients. Nevertheless, majoritarian electoral representation is not a requirement of civil disobedience. Consequently, a non-electoral reinterpretation of its representative function is necessary if civil disobedience is to count as any kind of representative act at all.

To this extent, I shall reinterpret civil disobedience as an exercise in non-electoral representative claim making (Saward 2006a, b, 2009, 2011). According to this conception, all kinds of claim makers – from politicians or 'spin doctors' to celebrities – can potentially be the legitimate representative of a constituency that they have discursively constructed. For instance, a politician might construct the national people as deeply concerned about immigration and so claim to represent this kind of popular concern in a national debate. Alternatively, a celebrity like Bono can claim to represent 'a lot of people in Africa,' constructing them as a constituency whose concerns would lead them to support his advocacy of particular global food aid policies. Of course, claiming to be representative in this sense does not guarantee that anyone is legitimately representative. Any such discursive claims to be representative are always contestable: they may be "accepted, rejected or ignored" (Saward 2009, 3). Hence, those constructed in some particular way by a representative claim must accept it as accurately depicting their shared concerns. This, however, presupposes that the constituency depicted in that way could also register their dissent from their portrayal. Indeed, lack of dissent does not register legitimacy when those depicted by the claim-maker have no resources, opportunity or fora in which to voice their rejection.

How does this conception of representative claim making apply to civil disobedience? Civil disobedients depict their public addressees as having particular kinds of concerns about justice. This much is apparent from altogether familiar remarks to the effect that they are the guardians of legitimacy (Habermas 1985) or that they represent the conscience of the nation or of humanity itself (Corlett 2003). The clear implication of any civilly disobedient act of public address is that the addressees are concerned about the same injustices that the disobedients are concerned about and that the latter claim to represent the constituency of addressees they have portrayed in this way. Indeed, this claim to represent the deepest concerns about justice of the addressees can potentially satisfy the legitimacy criteria for representative claim making insofar as it is eminently contestable. As invited to reconsider their present position, the addressees can accept or reject the notion that their actions violate justice. Good reasons are required to support the sincere belief of the disobedient representative claim makers that there is a fundamental injustice in the terms of social cooperation. If there are such reasons, this creates an obligation of justice for the addressees to undertake some appropriate reforms, unless they have better reasons to reject the disobedients' contention that the terms of cooperation are unjust.

If this analysis is correct, what difference does it make with respect to the question of disobedience promoting the cause of global distributive justice? It effectively detaches the idea of representing the perspective of moral concern about unfairness in the global economy from electoral representation. To be sure, this does not entirely sever the ties to voting and representation in liberal-democracies. As in my example above, the claim of the politician to represent the people's deep concerns about immigration may turn out to be a misrepresentation that results in subsequent electoral defeat. Democratic majoritarian voting may be the mechanism whereby representative claims are accepted or rejected. Nevertheless, it is not necessarily the only mechanism for accepting or rejecting claims. As long as there are alternative mechanisms for addressee to register acceptance or rejection, disobedient representative claim making may address global economic inequities. No longer exclusively reliant on majoritarian electoral processes, claims by disobedients to represent the perspective of concern about unfair terms of global cooperation may take many different forms, as I discuss the following sections.

5.3 Disobedience by Multinational Cosmopolitan Citizens from Liberal-Democracies

In his framework for civil disobedience, Rawls (1971) conceives of disobedients as *citizens*. Nevertheless, he clearly has in mind the national citizens of liberal-democratic states, not what I am calling *cosmopolitan citizens*: that is, citizens of the world who make cross-border appeals to principles of justice. I ask first whether disobedience by cosmopolitan citizens from different liberal-democratic states may prove consistent with this framework. Rather than proceeding straight to disobedience promoting global economic justice, I consider a hypothetical case of cross-border appeals to egalitarian principles of justice. These are principles shared by the peoples of liberal-democratic states but not by the peoples of traditional hierarchical states. For many contemporary civil rights activists in the US, denial of the transgender rights is a violation of equal civil liberties. Despite recent advances in the rights of LGBTQ persons such as the Supreme Court's 2015 decision in Obergefell v. Hodges to legalize marriage equality in all states, the rights of transgender persons remain insecure. As of 2017, the Court has returned appeals by transgender plaintiffs claiming discrimination at both state and local levels of government. Within Rawls' framework, however, discrimination against transgender persons may justify resort to civil disobedience. It may be justified in order to overcome deliberative inertia (Habermas 1985; Markovits 2005; Smith 2013), indeed motivating reconsideration through both official and public deliberation, concerning inegalitarian restrictions on transgender rights.

Nevertheless, transgender rights are not an exclusively national concern. They are the concern of anyone committed to those egalitarian principles of justice defining the moral character of liberal-democratic peoples. Would it, then, be appropriate for coalitions of transgender activists from, say, Belgium or Sweden to fly to the US with the intention of joining in – as cosmopolitan citizens – with the civil disobedience practices of transgender activists in the US? I think the answer to this has to be yes. By joining in the domestic disobedience campaign of American transgender activists, they might see themselves as providing some added impetus to its goal of overcoming deliberative inertia concerning transgender rights in the US. As a multinational coalition of cosmopolitan disobedients, their participation in the domestic campaign brings home to Americans the point that other liberal-democratic peoples share the commitments to egalitarian justice. Indeed, the input of this multinational coalition is itself a cause for the American people to reconsider. Moreover, the coalition may claim to represent the perspective of concern for the constituency of all citizens from liberal-democratic states with promoting egalitarian principles of justice.

This obviously cannot be reconciled with Rawls's restriction of disobedience to public address between co-nationals. Nevertheless, the coalition is surely justified in believing the American people is at fault from a shared standpoint of egalitarian social justice, and they surely are entitled to make an appropriately contestable claim to represent this multinational perspective of concern. Indeed, their claim to be representative of this shared perspective is contestable *in all such states* through their systems of electoral representation, as well as their institutions of the free speech and the free press. This, however, is subject to some important practical limitations. One such limitation is resource-based. Cross-border disobedience by cosmopolitan citizens assumes the possession of sufficient private resources to fly to the US and join in the practice of US disobedients. Some considerable level of resource is a precondition for the ability to participate in cross-border disobedience. Another kind of practical limitation could be its purported imprudence. After all, Rawls himself is adamant that disobedience should not overtax the capacities of a national majority to "handle dissent" (1971, 374), with the result that the intention of the disobedients becomes distorted.

Nevertheless, this sort of objection is not especially compelling. Not only are there some historical precedents for disobedience by cosmopolitan citizens, such as Gandhi's early civil disobedience campaigns in South Africa (Haksar 1976). There are also more recent examples of disobedience in a multinational cosmopolitan perspective, like that of the Indignacios in contemporary Europe (Bentouhami 2007). It is hardly a foregone conclusion that a multinational disobedience campaign would necessarily overtax the capacities of national peoples to handle dissent. Nevertheless, such a campaign would still depend on appeal to some broadly shared conception of justice. What, though, of the possibility of a multinational disobedience campaign, absent shared egalitarian commitments? A strong objection to this possibility might be that a campaign for transgender rights would make little or no sense in the case of a traditional-hierarchical society. That is, a society in which there is unlikely to be any indigenous campaign for transgender equality that affluent cosmopolitan citizens from liberal-democracies could join in. Indeed, within the borders of such a society, there is presumably no motivation to represent the perspective of concern for those denied transgender rights, as a vulnerable and discriminated group suffering injustice. To this extent, an influx of Belgians and Swedes making well-intentioned but culturally inappropriate disobedient claims to egalitarian justice would likely overtax the people's capacities to handle dissent. It would also raise difficult questions about respect for that people's moral character and autonomy (Beitz 2011).

The hypothetical case of a multinational disobedience campaign for transgender rights, however, focuses on a coalition of cosmopolitan citizens contesting *domestic justice in a particular society* of which they are not members. This, however, stands in contrast with multinational disobedience campaigns, which instead challenge the *regime of international justice*. Here, states representing peoples (not all of whom agree upon appropriate internal standards of domestic justice) delegate authority to the multiple and dispersed agencies of global governance. In this different context of international as opposed to domestic justice, the so-called global justice movement brings together diverse activists from around the world with a wide range of agendas. These agendas include demands for international action on climate change and opposition to the privatization of water. They also include opposition to patent laws on life-saving medications preventing the sale of cheap generics to poor countries, or the genetic codes of seeds thereby privatizing a natural public good used for millennia by subsistence farmers. All of the participants in such campaigns claim to represent some perspective of concern about injustice and unfairness in the present system of global governance. Often, the multinational participants in these campaigns protest the meetings of key agencies of global governance, such as WTO. Indeed, they sometimes resort to traditionally disobedient acts, like sit-ins or other forms of public obstruction, in countries of which they are not citizens.

Can, though, the participants in such disobedient protests targeting the agencies of global governance be inclusive of cosmopolitan citizens from traditional-hierarchical societies as well as liberal-democracies? I believe the answer to this question is yes. Nevertheless, all peoples sharing commitments to egalitarian social justice is not a plausible basis for an affirmative answer. Consequently, in the following section, I argue that it is best to conceive of the justificatory basis for multinational disobedience campaigns by cosmopolitan citizens for global justice, from both categories of society, absent any appeals to shared egalitarian commitments.

5.4 Disobedience by Multinational Cosmopolitan Citizens *Without* Egalitarianism

To be sure, cosmopolitan citizens from liberal-democracies may be inclined to justify multinational disobedience campaigns concerned with injustice and unfairness in the global system by appeal to the position known as global egalitarianism. This prescribes not only commitments to equalizing worldwide distributions of welfare and resources, but also of civil and political rights (for instance, Caney 2006). Here, global egalitarianism demands equal liberty and fair equality of opportunity for all persons in access to public offices, jobs, education, and so on (Cudd 2013). It also demands equal legal protections against discrimination, say, based on gender identifications, as in the above case of transgendered rights. To this extent, however, global egalitarianism would be an especially 'hard sell' to cosmopolitan citizens from traditional-hierarchical societies, for the reasons already given. By contrast, prioritarianism offers an alternative to global egalitarianism by stressing improvements to the position of the globally 'worst off,' via mechanisms such as a global difference principle (Beitz 1979) or global resource dividend (Pogge 1989). Nevertheless, Rawls himself in *Law of Peoples* (2001) explicitly rejects prioritarianism as tied to a global difference principle. He rejects it not because traditional-hierarchical peoples, in principle, are opposed to improving the situation of the globally worst off. That, after all, would contradict their commitments to securing basic economic security for those presently languishing in dire poverty, as an urgent human right (Ibid). Instead, consistent with Rawls' *Theory* (1971), prioritizing the situation of the worst off via such global redistribution programs remains tied to the egalitarian goal of achieving a 'fair value' of liberty among all persons.

As distinct from egalitarianism and prioritarianism, sufficientarianism emphasizes the satisfaction of basic needs for subsistence and shelter, along with international guarantees of freedom from subservience, as sufficient for global justice. This alternative to egalitarianism and prioritarianism does not assume any shared egalitarian commitments among participants in global disobedience campaigns from different societies with different conceptions of domestic – rather than international – justice. Instead, sufficientarianism contents itself with realizing minimal standards globally for leading a decent human life (Buchanan 2007; also see Nagel 2005; Miller 2012): feeding the hungry, ensuring access to elementary health care, and effective legal redress before domestic or international agencies, should minimal or sufficientarian standards go unmet. To this extent, sufficientarianism appears to align with the special class of urgent human rights in *Law of Peoples*. It thus provides a viable legitimation basis for global civil disobedience absent the egalitarian social justice commitments of liberal-democratic peoples. At any rate, this follows as long as the characteristic disobedience campaigns of the global justice movement fit into the mold of upholding minimal standards of subsistence and non-subservience for the global poor.

Climate justice and the reform of international patent law, for instance, are quite plausibly conditions for realizing the range of urgent human rights laid out in *Law of Peoples*. Indeed, cosmopolitan citizens from traditional-hierarchical societies could join in global disobedience campaigns with their counterparts from liberal-democracies. They could do so to the extent such campaigns remain content with advancing minimal sufficientarian standards that do not threaten the international legitimacy of inegalitarian domestic consultation hierarchies that honor international agreements on acceptable emissions standards for CO_2 and place action on preventable morbidity over corporate profits. Nevertheless, sufficientarianism is not the only option for justifying collaborative global disobedience campaigns among cosmopolitan citizens from both traditional-hierarchical and liberal-democratic societies. Here, I appeal to Rawls' notion of a global egalitarianism *between peoples* and not individual persons. My claim, then, is that such a coalition of disobedient cosmopolitan citizens should seek justification for their campaigns in violations of equal liberty and fair equality of opportunity between peoples as engaged in international cooperation.

This approach appeals to Rawls' idea of liberty's fair value. Applied to individual persons as citizens in *Theory* (1971), the fair value of liberty entails that those similarly endowed and motivated should have similar opportunities for self-determination, regardless of how rich or poor they are. The fair value of liberty, however, presupposes a well-ordered constitutional society that effectively guarantees the basic political liberties of its citizens to hold office, influence elections, and so on. Indeed, citizens use these equal liberties of political participation to shape fair terms of cooperation, thus protecting themselves against injustices of harassment and exploitation to which they might otherwise be vulnerable. Injustices of harassment and exploitation derive from asymmetries of wealth and social power between citizens. Consequently, Rawls contends that liberty's fair value will ensure that economic inequality – along with its potential to create such injustices – will not get out of hand (1971, 363). In this regard, he argues that an *unfair value of liberty*, or piecewise distribution of rights and opportunities for political participation, may well justify civil disobedience. One compelling reason why it may do so is that economic inequality has got out of hand in the absence of liberty's fair value and the ability of citizens effectively to protect themselves from exploitation.

To be sure, Rawls does not explicitly apply the fair value of political participation doctrine to liberal-democratic and hierarchical peoples in *Law of Peoples* (2001). Nevertheless, his intention is clearly that both categories of people, as similarly endowed and motivated, should enjoy a fair value of rights and opportunities for self-determination in international cooperation. Here, I contend that a 'fair value' of liberty for peoples is realized when the terms of international cooperation are no longer functions of asymmetries of power and influence between rich and poor countries. That is, such a value is realized when cooperation is no longer a function of asymmetries of power and influence, based on population size, territory size, natural or financial resources, and so on (Rawls 2001). Indeed, the fair value of self-determination for peoples is a condition for their being able to protect themselves from injustices of harassment and exploitation derived from existing global economic inequalities. These may be injustices of poor countries being harassed into, say, accepting economic Structural Adjustment Programs (SAPs) in return for IMF loans or being sanctioned for their own protectionist policies while also being expected to pay import tariffs to rich and powerful countries hypocritically and exploitatively sanctioning them.

All in all, injustices of harassment and exploitation resulting from asymmetries of power and influence between rich and poor countries in international cooperation are sufficiently 'out of hand' to justify disobedience among cosmopolitan citizens from *all* decent societies committed to respect for the autonomy and sovereignty of peoples. Here, there is no issue of lack of respect for the autonomy of particular peoples, as in the earlier case of a multinational cross-border disobedience campaign for transgendered rights. The difference is that the fair value of self-determination for poor and rich countries alike in the global economy is uncontroversially a requirement of the shared decency standard. In the next section, I extend this argument from coalitions of disobedient cosmopolitan citizens from both liberal-democratic and traditional-hierarchical societies to disobedient peoples of both such societies. In this respect, I turn to the different but related case of inter-state disobedience between peoples represented by state officials, in international negotiations and tribunals.

5.5 Disobedience by Peoples of Different States

My contention is that there is nothing like a fair value of liberty between rich and poor peoples of the world and that global economic inequities are indeed out of hand. To this extent, poor countries are often not to blame for their failures to satisfy the urgent material needs of their peoples, lifting themselves out of poverty. Instead, global poverty is, in some significant part, the collective responsibility-failure of the richest and most powerful states. Indeed, it is their failure insofar as they have wielded their power and influence to organize international cooperation based on unfair and exploitative rules, favoring their economic interests over those of the poorest and least developed members of the international community. While they are not solely responsible for this circumstance of global injustice, liberal-democratic states are certainly among its leading culprits. Consequently, any liberal democratic state could be justified in resorting to internationally disobedient public address challenging such unfairness and calling upon all other states and their peoples to reconsider their present stance concerning the terms of cooperation between rich and poor Peoples. A rather obvious case of challenging the unfairness of existing terms through international civil disobedience can be found in the state of Brazil deciding to produce and export generic HIV medications in defiance of intellectual property rights, protected under existing international law (Allen 2011, 2015; also see Kokaz 2005; Goodin 2005).

Indeed, violating unfair international law, Brazil may be said have represented – at an official state-level – the belief of the Brazilian People that existing rules on intellectual property rights are unfair and exploitative. Perfectly good reasons can be given for this believe insofar as such rules leave some of the poorest peoples of the world without access to affordable life-saving medications. Nevertheless, officials of the state of Brazil may also be said to represent the conscience of all others states and peoples for whom the protection under international law of profits over lives is unacceptable. On the one hand, it is unacceptable to the Brazilian people and all other decent peoples because it violates the urgent human rights of persons. But, on the other hand, it is unacceptable because profits over lives is a function of a system of exploitative cooperation in which the poorest peoples lack any effective participatory is shaping these rules. In other words, profits over lives is a function of the unfair value of liberty between peoples. Consequently, Brazilian state officials make contestable representative claims portraying the Brazilian people and all other peoples as concerned about fairness in the terms of cooperation for all peoples. These claims are contestable electorally in Brazil or in any other liberal-democratic country whose officials might reject Brazil's claim represent the conscience of humanity by representing their peoples differently as concerned about the primacy of international law.

Indeed, this model of international civil disobedience and international representative claim making remains broadly consistent with Rawls. At any rate, it remains consistent with his emphasis on disobedience as promoting fair rules as a way to obstruct injustices of harassment and exploitation. Nevertheless, can unelected officials accurately represent tradition-hierarchical peoples as sharing a perspective of concern about global inequity? The answer is unproblematically yes, as long the representative claims of such officials are suitably contestable by the people they purport to represent, despite the absence of domestic institutions of electoral representation. Such claims meet this condition, however, insofar as contestability is a function of consultation protocols assuring the hierarchically ordered people a participatory voice in providing appropriate feedback on the accuracy of official representative claim making. If, for instance, officials represent them as more concerned with profits than with lives, where this is clearly in violation of their common good conception of justice, then the people may legitimately reject this depiction of themselves. Moreover, the ruling elite would be obliged to change the way in which it represented the concerns of the people. It would be obliged to do so in that its own legitimacy depends on its ability to explain its judgments specifically in light of this shared conception of justice.

Consequently, official claim makers from both categories of society – traditional-hierarchical as well as liberal-democratic – *are equal* with respect to representing the moral right their own people to disobey the present rules of international cooperation. In other words, no one category is any more authoritative than the other is, when it comes to internationally disobedient representative claim making. Traditional-hierarchical peoples bind by justice liberal-democratic peoples to give uptake for internationally disobedient public address, and vice versa. Indeed, representing an international perspective of concern about global inequities, states and peoples take on the role of disobedient 'cosmopolitan citizens.' Moreover, in doing so, they embrace a moderate cosmopolitanism about international justice (Scheffler 1999; also see Buchanan 2007). Here, internationally disobedient acts are cosmopolitan because they acknowledge duties of justice beyond their own territorial borders, concerning the special class of urgent human rights. Nevertheless, these cosmopolitan duties are moderate because they are compatible with upholding the normative priority of states and peoples, where each owe the others a fair value of liberty in shaping the rules of international cooperation. Such a fair value of political participation in international rule making among all decent peoples – as disobedient cosmopolitan citizens – aims to keep *in hand* those injustices attributable to asymmetries of wealth and resources.

5.6 Ongoing Controversy over Global Inequities

I have argued that the unfair value of liberty between peoples is the primary justification for cross border disobedience by coalitions of cosmopolitan citizens from different states and different states themselves as cosmopolitan citizens. In this respect, I have distinguished it from global egalitarianism and prioritarianism as alternate possible justificatory bases for such disobedience. I have already indicated that global egalitarianism would be a hard sell to traditional-hierarchical peoples and that prioritarianism is equally problematic for such peoples to the extent it remains tied to promoting egalitarian ideals. Nevertheless, my approach does not rule out either global egalitarianism or prioritarianism as possible bases for a reformed system of international cooperation between peoples. After all, it is conceivable that controversies over the global reach and applicability of egalitarian ideals, and the relationship of prioritarianism to these ideals, could be resolved in the due course of time. Those are, above all, controversies to be worked out in ongoing global public discourse. Indeed, they are controversies in the sense that decent peoples may reasonably disagree about their appropriateness and applicability to the global domain of politics.

By contrast, the virtue of appealing to the unfair value of liberty between peoples under the present terms of international cooperation is that it is *uncontroversial*. Indeed, decent peoples cannot reasonably disagree that all other decent peoples ought to enjoy a fair value of liberty in shaping international negotiations over how to appropriately reform a system of cooperation underwriting the harassment and exploitation of the poor. To this extent, global egalitarianism and prioritarianism certainly count as possibilities of reform that the international community may consider. However, they remain controversial justificatory grounds for disobedience motivating global public reconsideration and deliberation over the various possibilities of reform. By contrast, sufficientarianism, as opposed to global egalitarianism and prioritarianism, is an uncontroversial justificatory ground. Moreover, it provides reasons for uptake and reconsideration by the global public every bit as compelling as the unfair value of liberty between rich and poor peoples.

Indeed, sufficientarianism contained no more than a minimal component of economic justice, prescribing non-controversially that no persons should die from the failure to meet urgent needs for food, shelter, and so on. Consequently, no decent people could reasonably disagree about meeting such a minimal sufficientarian standard. This much is true. Hence, consistent with my earlier appeal in Chap. 2 to Scanlon's principle of reasonable rejection, no decent people could *reasonably reject* disobedient calls to reconsider based on either the unfair value of liberty between peoples or the failure of the international system to secure minimal sufficientarian standards for all persons. Does, then, this mean that there is parity between the unfair value of liberty between peoples in international negotiations over terms of global economic cooperation and the failure of the global system to meet sufficientarian standards, as justificatory grounds for disobedience? My answer is no.

It is no for at least two reasons. The first is that the satisfaction of minimal sufficientarian standards will likelier than not be a function of the fair value of liberty between peoples. Rawls' original contention from *Theory* (1971) was that the fair value of liberty is a condition for poor citizens protecting themselves from harassment and exploitation by rich citizens. By extension to the international domain, the fair value of liberty between peoples is a condition for poor peoples protecting themselves from harassment and exploitation by rich peoples. The second reason is that the fair value of liberty between peoples can be detached from sufficientarianism. Liberty's fair value in reconsidering the terms of international economic cooperation might resolve in shared commitments to sufficientarian standards. Nevertheless, as indicated immediately above, it might also resolve ultimately in shared commitments to the considerably more demanding standards of egalitarianism or prioritarianism. My point, then, is that there is no need to tie cross border disobedience into any one or other proposal for reform of the international economic system. Instead, it is enough that moderate cosmopolitan disobedients of one kind or another should base their calls to reconsider the terms of international cooperation on grounds that no decent peoples can reasonably reject. Indeed, the unfair value of liberty between peoples, and not individual persons, provide such grounds.

5.7 Conclusion

In this chapter, my focus of attention shifted from undocumented persons, as disobedient actors, living and working in the domestic systems of cooperation of both liberal and hierarchical societies, to global economic inequities, representing perspectives of concern about the latter, and the fair equality of liberty between peoples. Indeed, in discussing the plight of the undocumented, I argued for a human right to be a political participation, wherever you are. By contrast, I did not argue in this chapter of any novel addition to the list of human rights embraced by decent peoples. The reason for this difference should be obvious enough. The decency commitments of peoples already entail, at least, minimal standards of economic subsistence, such that the hungry ought to be fed, wherever they are in the world. To that extent, urgent poverty relief and economic development are already human rights. Moreover, the right of the global poor to be political participants has little application in the present context of debate. As I have argued, they lack the resources to become effective political participants in global politics. Consequently, the mode of political participation through disobedient public address is representative in the double sense of representing both the perspective of concern of all decent peoples for the global poor and, more importantly, concern for the fair value of liberty between rich and poor peoples. Indeed, these perspectives of concern are represented to the global public by affluent cosmopolitan citizens or states.

Here, the primary work of justifying resort to disobedience is accomplished through the idea of the fair value of liberty for peoples, rather than persons as holders of individual human rights. This approach is consistent with Rawls' emphasis in *Law of Peoples* (2001) on creating orderliness, in response to global economic inequity, rather than global resource transfers, on the models of egalitarianism, prioritarianism, or sufficientarianism. To be sure, the global system is only peicewise just when some but not all inhabitants of the planet have access to adequate nutrition, necessary medicines, shelter, and so on. Consequently, it is disordered to the extent these conditions go unfulfilled. Nevertheless, it is even more profoundly disordered when the peicewise just character of the global system is a function of the unfair value of liberty in shaping the terms of global cooperation. It is more profoundly disordered to the extent that a well ordered system would empower all peoples to exercise the fair value of their liberty in shaping these terms, in light of their own goals for national economic self-development (Miller 2012). Resource transfers in the absence of a fair value of liberty between peoples run the risk of resolving one form of disorder, while leaving another in place. Even assuming it resolves the problems of global poverty by assuring access to nutrition, shelter, etc., a global transfer scheme that does not simultaneous address the unfair value of liberty between peoples would violate international decency, prescribing the equality of self-determining peoples. Indeed, I argued in Chap. 1 that decency is an idea of non-domination between peoples. Nevertheless, non-domination entails a fair value of liberty; consequently, resource transfers in the absence of such a fair value between peoples amounts to the domination by rich of poor peoples.

This analysis takes seriously Rawls' proposition from *A Theory of Justice* (1971) that civil disobedience is justified in response to fundamental violations of liberty. Indeed, as long as the equal liberties and their fair value are guaranteed, economic inequalities will not get out of hand, thus maintaining good order in the system of cooperation. Here, I interpret Rawls as saying that appropriate measures to keep inequalities in hand will be taken, provided that economic policies are shaped through inclusive processes of public communication or deliberation (Lefkowitz 2007). My argument, then, is that the civil disobedience of cosmopolitan citizens and states should mimic this justificatory rationale. In other words, disobedience is justified because of the unfair value of liberty between rich and poor peoples, in shaping the terms of the global system. Nevertheless, the analysis is complicated in that effective disobedience campaigns, in the global domain, require the possession of resources; hence, my stress on the representative function of affluent cosmopolitan citizens and state. Indeed, an advocate for resource transfers might object that fair value cannot be achieved without first closing the inequality gap and so transferals are a necessary presupposition of ever achieving a fair value of liberty between peoples.

From the point of view of my concern with justifying disobedience by cosmopolitan citizens and states, however, fair value has to take *justificatory precedence*. That is, it takes justificatory precedence, as the primary ground for disobedience. Global economic inequities are symptomatic of disorder in the global system. Indeed, the normative significance of such inequities is considerable insofar as they may signal failures to secure basic human rights. Nevertheless, the principal source of responsibility-taking for human rights is states and peoples. Consequently, the justification for disobedience is quite properly the creation of an orderly system of cooperation between peoples. All peoples are owed a fair value of liberty in determining rules of international cooperation, along with due respect for their sovereign rights to determine those policies they determine to be in their own best interest from within the general parameters of decency and human rights. This approach permits a global perspective on civil disobedience to the extent the fair value of liberty is an uncontroversial justificatory ground for both liberal-democratic and traditional-hierarchical peoples.

Overall, the approach entails a reinterpretation of the duty to give assistance to the poor. Under the condition in which the global system is only piecewise just and disordered, human rights advice is not enough to fulfil this duty. Indeed, the duty to assist the global poor by creating a more orderly global system of cooperation also encompasses diverse disobedient protest calling for all decent peoples to reconsider existing international rules in ways that respect the fair value of liberty between peoples. The reformulation of such rules is a matter for open ended global public discourse, leading to reformed international agreements. To this extent, my discussion has not included proposals for such reform. My concern has been exclusively with the appropriate justificatory ground for disobedience as underwriting campaigns by cosmopolitan citizens and states from across the very different outlooks on justice of liberal-democratic and traditional-hierarchical peoples.

References

Allen, Michael. 2011. Civil Disobedience, International. In *Encyclopedia of Global Justice*, ed. Deen Chatterjee, vol. 1, 133–135. Dordrecht: Springer.

———. 2015. Civil Disobedience in Cosmopolitan Perspective: National Responsibility, Citizenship, Representation. In *Cosmopolitanism and the Legacies of Dissent*, ed. Tamara Caraus and Camil Parvu. New York: Routledge.

Beitz, Charles. 2008. Justice and International Relations. In *Global Justice Seminal Essays*, ed. Thomas Pogge and Darrel Moellendorf. St. Paul: Paragon House.

———. 2011. *The Idea of Human Rights*. Oxford: Oxford University Press.

Bentouhami, Hourya. 2007. Civil Disobedience from Thoreau to Transnational Mobilizations: The Global Challenge. *Essays in Philosophy* 8(2): Article 3.

Blake, Michael. 2001. Distributive Justice, State Coercion, and Autonomy. *Philosophy and Public Affairs* 30(3): 257–296.

Brock, Gillian. 2005. Egalitarianism, Ideals and Cosmopolitan Justice. *Social Philosophy and Policy* 5: 143–168.

Buchanan, Allen. 2007. *Justice, Legitimacy and Self-Determination*. Oxford: Oxford University Press.

Caney, Simon. 2006. *Justice beyond Borders: A Global Political Theory*. Oxford: Oxford University Press.

Corlett, Angelo. 2003. *Terrorism: A Philosophical Analysis*. Dordrecht: Springer.

Cudd, Ann. 2013. Human Rights and Global Equal Opportunity: Inclusion not Provision. In *Human Rights: The Hard Cases*, ed. Cindy Holder and David Reidy, 193–208. Cambridge: Cambridge University Press.

Habermas, Jurgen. 1985. *Theory of Communicative Action*. Vol. 1. Boston: Beacon Press.

Haksar, Vinit. 1976. Rawls and Gandhi on Civil Disobedience. *Inquiry* 19: 151–192.

Held, David. 2004. *The Global Covenant: The Social Democratic Alternative to the Washington Consensus*. Cambridge: Polity Press.

Lefkowitz, David. 2007. On a Moral Right to Civil Disobedience. *Ethics* 117(2): 202–233.

Loriaux, Sylvie. 2012. Fairness in International Economic Cooperation: Moving beyond Rawls' Duty of Assistance. *Critical Review of International Social and Political Philosophy* 15(1): 19–39.

Markovits, Daniel. 2005. Democratic Disobedience. *Yale Law Journal* 114: 1898–1948.

Miller, David. 2005. Against Global Egalitarianism. *Journal of Ethics* 9(1/2): 55–79.

———. 2012. *National Responsibility and Global Justice*. Oxford: Oxford University Press.

Moellendorf, Darrel. 2008. Constructing the Law of Peoples. In *Global Justice: Seminar Essays*, ed. Thomas Pogge and Darrel Moellendorf, 461–580. St. Paul: Paragon House.

Nagel, Thomas. 2005. The Problem of Global Justice. *Philosophy and Public Affairs* 33(2): 113–147.
Ogunye, Temi. 2015. Global Justice and Transnational Civil Disobedience. *Ethics and Global Politics* 8(1): 27217. Published Online 24 June 2015.
Pitkin, Hannah. 1972. *The Concept of Representation*. Berkeley: University of California Press.
Pogge, Thomas. 1989. *Realizing Rawls*. New York: Cornell University Press.
———. 2008. Cosmopolitanism and Sovereignty. In *Global Justice: Seminal Essays*, ed. Thomas Pogge and Darrel Moellendorf, 355–390. St. Paul: Paragon House.
Rawls, John. 1971. *A Theory of Justice*. Cambridge, MA: Harvard University Press.
———. 2001. *The Law of Peoples*. Cambridge, MA: Harvard University Press.
Reidy, David. 2007. A Just Global Economy: A Defense of Rawls. *The Journal of Ethics* 11: 193–236.
Risse, Mathias. 2015. *On Global Justice*. Princeton: Princeton University Press.
Saward, Michael. 2006a. In Place of Global Democracy. *Ethical Perspectives* 15(4): 506–526.
———. 2006b. The Representative Claim. *Contemporary Political Theory* 5(3): 297–318.
———. 2009. Authorization and Authenticity: Representation and the Unelected. *Journal of Political Philosophy* 9(3): 1–22.
———. 2011. Slow Theory: Taking Time over Transnational Representation. *Ethics and Global Politics* 4(1): 1–18.
Scheffler, Samuel. 1999. Conceptions of Cosmopolitanism. *Utilitas* 11: 255–276.
Walzer, Michael. 1999. International Society: What Is the Best That We Can Do? *Ethical Perspectives* 6: 201–210.

Chapter 6
Executive Prerogative and Disobedient Disclosure of Government Secrets

Abstract In this chapter, I look at two distinct and conflicting modes of disobedient action. On the one hand, secretive resort by governments to discretionary extra-legal actions in order to preserve the people and, on the other hand, the disobedient disclosure of such actions by cosmopolitan citizens. Indeed, as cosmopolitan citizens, 'disobedient disclosers' have an equal claim to justification in resorting to discretionary extra-legality. They do so by virtue of the non-publicity of government prerogative. Consequently, governments and disclosers make competing and contradictory claims to be justified in going beyond the mandates of existing law. This, however, is not a dilemma can be resolved by appeal to an addition to the minimalist list of urgent human rights in Law of Peoples, such as an urgent human right to government transparency. That, after all, would validate one justifiable claim to decency while contradicting another. Instead, decency requires the protection of diverse and sometimes contradictory disobedient actions. Nevertheless, this does not entail immunity from the legal consequences for disobedience. It points not to a human right to transparency as to leniency for diverse disobedience each with a valid claim to the justifiability of their actions. Here, leniency for government officials and disobedient disclosers is a mandate of reasonableness among decent peoples, responding to the irreducible complexity of politics.

6.1 Introduction

Constitutional government advances an ideal of the non-arbitrary rule of law, as opposed to the arbitrary, extra-legal discretionary rule of a tyrant. Nonetheless, almost all constitutionalists acknowledge the necessity and legitimacy of, at least, some resort to extra-legal discretion, whether by the executive power of government or by citizens who constitute government for their mutual advantage and self-preservation. In the case of the executive, Locke's idea of the prerogative captures the necessity and legitimacy of

M. Allen, *Civil Disobedience in Global Perspective*,
Studies in Global Justice 16, DOI 10.1007/978-94-024-1164-5_6

such resort to extra-legality (1988). In the case of citizens, Rawls' idea of civil disobedience captures the legitimacy of resort to discretionary action against the law (1971). In both cases, extra-legal discretion expresses *fidelity* to the constitutional ideal of the rule of law. In the case of civil disobedience, such fidelity is already widely acknowledged. In the case of executive prerogative, however, such acknowledgment is less forthcoming. Extra-legal discretion by the executive smacks of the most serious of political crimes for constitutionalists: tyranny. Consequently, any claims made by the executive to exercise a right and duty of prerogative are viewed with extreme suspicion.

This holds true with respect to the increasing resort of post governments since 9/11 to executive prerogative, in response to national security emergencies (for instance, Neocleous 2007). Revelations through investigative journalism, leaks, and disclosures, that the executive has deliberately concealed its use of prerogative from public view and scrutiny compound suspicions. When the executive power conceals its uses of prerogative from such scrutiny, how can the public know that its acts are good rather than harmful? A notable recent example of suspicion turning to disobedient action is Edward Snowden's disclosure of the NSA's PRISM program involving the mass collection of the meta-data of U.S. citizens. To be sure, the executive can always justify its concealed uses of prerogative for national security reasons in a program like PRISM following the disobedient act of disclosure. Nevertheless, the very idea of an executive, in Locke's words, acting "without or even against law" (1988, 174) behind the backs of the people raises profound fears that the legitimacy of the constitutional order may itself be in question. It may be in question because publicity is ultimately the guarantee of the people's freedom from subordination to the arbitrary judgments of the executive, as tyrannical prince. This indeed makes the case of executive prerogative seem quite different from that of civil disobedience, in which citizens resort to extra-legality, as a form of public address defined by publicity and openness to popular scrutiny and judgment. It is, then, small wonder that the legitimacy of extra-legal discretion by disobedient citizens is easier to acknowledge and accept than such discretion by the executive power of government, especially when the latter exercises this power secretively.

Nonetheless, any justificatory advantage of publicity enjoyed by civil disobedience may be lost when citizens resort to extra-legal discretion in order to disclose the concealed uses of executive prerogative. After all, publicity in this context potentially exposes the people to risks to life, limb, and property that the executive may well be attempting to preserve them against in resorting to prerogative. Moreover, it may be that the disobedient disclosure of concealed uses of executive prerogative itself contradicts the ideal of a government constituted by the people expressly for their collective self-preservation. To this extent, disobedient disclosures of such uses of the prerogative are every bit as problematic as the prerogative. That is, as different kinds of resort to extra-legal discretion, disobedient disclosure and concealed uses of executive prerogative do not align with the ideal of constitutionalism as much as they are both in some considerable tension with it. Neither would appear to be clearly and unambiguously expressions of fidelity to constitutional order.

In what follows, however, I shall argue that both can be such expressions. Indeed, both can express such fidelity insofar as both have principled justifications, appealing to the same fundamental principles of constitutionalism, and in much the same kind of justificatory situation. In this light, I contend that there is a remarkably close conceptual alignment of executive prerogative and its disobedient disclosure, from the standpoint of their justifications. Here, I use the term 'disobedient disclosure' in a special and restrictive sense. In particular, I use it to establish a contrast between leaking, as a self-interested act of disclosure for political gain, and whistleblowing, as a public-spirited act of exposing malfeasance or misconduct (Delmas 2015; Scheuerman 2014; Sager 2013). This contrast with leaking should be obvious enough. Constitutional patriotism, that is, fidelity to constitutional principles, motivates a disobedient discloser, such as Snowden (Greenwald 2014; also see Muller 2007), and not a narrow concern with advancing a self-interested agenda. As for whistleblowing, this is different from a disobedient disclosure in my sense insofar as the latter does not necessarily expose malfeasance or misconduct. A disobedient discloser may believe that malfeasance is exposed, but that is not what matters from the justificatory point of view.

As a further point of clarification, I stress that disclosure should not be taken to "mean access to all information without restraint" (Birkinshaw 2006). For them to satisfy general conditions of ethical justifiability, disclosures are always subject to qualifications, such as the redaction of the names in cases in which publicity may endanger lives (for a general discussion of the morality of disclosure, see Bouville 2008). That said, however, a disobedient disclosure of concealed use of executive prerogative is potentially justifiable, even on the assumption that the executive may have been right in resorting to such use of prerogative. This latter point is vital to my argument as holding open the possibility of both forms of extra-legal discretion being justified. Nevertheless, such a conceptual alignment with respect to their justification inevitably raises the following question. How can the concealed use of prerogative and its disobedient disclosure both be objectively justifiable expressions of fidelity to the constitutional order? In other words, how can they both be justifiable when the discloser cancels out the executive's efforts to preserve the people against what it believes to be genuine existential risks to life, limb, and property? Consequently, an account must be given of how both forms of resort to extra-legal discretion, by executive and disclosers respectively, can be embraced as justifiable, despite their potentially operating at cross-purposes with one another

Why is it important to give such an account? Without demonstrating how both can be expressions of constitutional fidelity, it is too easy for critics of extra-legal discretion by the executive power to collapse the distinction between prerogative and tyranny. This may delegitimize the prerogative, with some undesirable consequences. For instance, delegitimation may hobble future efforts by executives to perform the function of preserving the people against genuine existential threats. Alternatively, it may encourage the executive power to become ever more secretive and resistant to any possibility of popular scrutiny of its discretionary judgments, perhaps making a self-fulfilling prophecy of the descent from constitutionalism into tyranny. Nevertheless, the fact that the absence of any compelling account of how both forms of extra-legality can be justifiable also makes it too easy for the critics of disobedient disclosure to deny the legitimacy of citizens publicizing what the executive wants to keep hidden from public view. Here, the delegitimization of disclosure by conscientiously motivated citizens may prove equally deleterious for the constitutional order. The executive may become too comfortable with exercising its discretionary judgment, sliding into arbitrariness and tyranny, if disclosure is out of bounds, as a legitimate and justifiable form of civil disobedience.

In the interest of maintaining focus on the justifiability of extra-legal discretion, I shall not be concerned in this article with the question of legal reform. This might be surprising, given that civil disobedience has a reformist agenda (Rawls 1971). By seeking to institutionalize transparency and accountability rules for executive discretion, whistleblowers and disobedient disclosers likewise have an agenda for legal reform. Indeed, there is already a sizable public policy literature discussing possible reforms to tame executive discretion (see for instance the papers collected in Hood and Heald 2006; also see Fenster 2012). I by no means wish to downplay the importance of this literature. Nevertheless, I want instead to take seriously the idea motivating Locke's discussion of prerogative: that rules cannot encompass all contingencies so that the justifiability extra-legality by the executive always remains an open possibility.

Moreover, I restrict my discussion of civil disobedience to the general framework of justification laid out by Rawls (1971), even though there are several other models of civil disobedience in the recent political philosophy literature (notable recent exceptions to this literature include Markovits 2005; Lovell 2009; Brownlee 2012; Smith 2013). Nevertheless, these contributions often stress the possibilities of justification at some distance from fidelity to constitutional principles. So, for instance, its justification may be given less in terms of such fidelity and more in terms of its role in improving democratic public deliberation (Smith 2013); or, it may be detached from constitutionalism entirely and linked instead to justificatory criteria from environmental philosophy (Welchman 2001). Indeed, aside from these recent contributions, civil disobedience has also long been associated with comprehensive religious and metaphysical justification as in the activism of King and Gandhi. Nevertheless, my discussion offers a secular argument, freestanding of comprehensive and metaphysical assumptions. Consequently, stressing constitutional fidelity over other considerations, the Rawlsian framework is the most appropriate one for my purposes in this article, even though it has to undergo some significant adaptations in order to deal with what I am calling disobedient disclosure.

I proceed in the following steps. I first discuss his concept of the prerogative and its place in his constitutional theory, as well as its connection to civil disobedience. I then develop a reinterpretation of civil disobedience in light of disobedient disclosures, before going on to field some problems with this reinterpretation. Dismissing the claim that disobedient disclosure is supported by a human right to know (Birkinshaw 2006), I focus instead on the question of penalizing executives and disclosers in light of an obligation for decent, reasonable peoples to show appropriate leniency for executive and disclosers. Finally, I extend my analysis from its origin in liberal constitutionalism to the international community of all decent peoples. This places it in a properly global perspective grounded in ideas of decency and moderate cosmopolitanism, as developed in earlier chapters.

6.2 Lockean Prerogative

Why begin with an historical exegesis of Locke? Indeed, Locke may seem far removed from my concern with discretionary acts of post-9/11 governments. Nevertheless, he is relevant to my discussion insofar as he gives a clear justification for the executive power of a constitutional order resorting to extra-legality. In this respect, a brief consideration of him should help to dispel the false idea that an executive who departs from the rule of law is necessarily doing the wrong thing. Here, I stress two features of Locke's thought. The first is that he attributes an original executive power of interpreting the law of nature to justify actions taken for self-preservation and mutual advantage to the people themselves. Only then is such an original power of the people transferred to the executive power of government to act as arbiter of how to interpret the law of nature, in cases of controversy. Crucially, though, the people do not give up their original executive power, but rather hold it in reserve should the government ever rebel against them by ruling against their public good. That they may reclaim their power to interpret what is necessary for their self-preservation and advantage from the executive will later prove important for my defense of disobedient disclosure. As for the second feature, this is that – as popularly authorized interpreter of the law of nature – the executive power of government can be justified in departing from the rule of law, *without* acting arbitrarily or tyrannically. How can this be so?

Locke's reasoning is quite simple. Granting a separation of powers between a legislative and executive branch, "the good of society requires, that several things should be left to the discretion of him, that has the Executive Power." This follows in that the people's legislators are not "able to foresee and provide, by Laws, for all, that may be useful to the Community." Consequently, the "Executor of the Laws, having the power in his hands, has by the common Law of Nature, a right to make use of it, for the good of the Society." He goes on to gloss this right of the executive by saying that those things "which the law can by no means provide for … must necessarily be left" to the executive's discretion "to be ordered by him, as the publick good and advantage shall require." To this extent, he insists it is "fit that the Laws themselves should in some Cases give way to the Executive Power, or rather to this Fundamental Law of Nature and Government, *viz*, That as much as may be, *all* the Members of Society are to be preserved" (1988, 174–175). Indeed, acknowledging the epistemic limitations of law making and the indeterminacy of the future, Locke contends that extra-legal discretion may be justified in virtue of the power of the executive to interpret the law of nature for the "Publick good." This, of course, is the power of interpretation and discretionary judgment originally transferred to it by the people. Such a transfer of power locates the executive's right of prerogative in the center of his constitutional theory, effectively distinguishing it from arbitrariness and tyranny.

Locke then positively defines the prerogative as "*nothing but the Power of doing publick good without a Rule*" (1988, 378). Therefore, he says it is justifiable to "pull down an Innocent Man's House to stop the Fire, when the next to it is burning" (Ibid), despite a constitutional rule binding the executive to respect private property. To this extent, he strongly emphasizes the relevance of the good conscience and "sincerity" in justifying extra-legal discretion by the executive (Neocleous 2007, 137 & 139). Here, the central role he assigns to conscientiousness and sincerity in his definition of the prerogative leads to a close conceptual alignment with the definition of civil disobedience, which I explore further in the following section. Just as the sincerity of the executive exercising its right of prerogative serves to distinguish it from the arbitrary judgment of a tyrant doing public harm without a rule, the conscientiousness of citizens exercising their right to civil disobedience distinguishes them from mere criminals, breaking rules only for personal gain and without regard for shared political principle (Rawls 1971). Indeed, both forms of extra-legality derive their justification in part from their sincere or conscientious character. But this stress on justification by sincerity of conviction, when resorting to extra-legality, is *only* part of the story. The other part consists in being subject to public scrutiny and judgment, where the prerogative is as much subject to the latter as civil disobedience.

The demand that its justification demands should be subject to public scrutiny and judgment is often overlooked by post-9/11 critics who mistakenly see Locke as denying the secular objectivity of any such justification (see Neocleous 2007; for a contrasting sympathetic views of the prerogative in Locke's constitutionalism, see Fatovic 2001 and Mattie 2005). Here, such critics respond to Locke's own assertion that there can be "no Judge on Earth" as to whether the prerogative "is made right use of," and that "there is no remedy in this … but to Appeal to Heaven" (1988, 179). Hence, on this false interpretation, "Locke's advice is: start praying" for "divine intervention" (Rehfeld 2008). Nevertheless, there is good reason to dismiss the idea that Locke himself rejected the possibility of an objective secular judgment of executive prerogative. Seen in light of the people's retention of their own executive power and their right to exercise it in resistance to arbitrariness and tyranny, Locke should be understood as allowing that it is legitimate for the people to "trust [their] own judgment" (Rehfeld 2008, 72). In other words, the people judge right use of the prerogative and not God. In this respect, the people's judgment of whether or not the executive power of government judged rightly in resorting to prerogative appeals to another principle defining the proper end or aim of constitutional government. Complementary to the principle that 'all Members should be preserved,' this indeed is the principle that no "Rational Creature … when free" can "put himself into Subjection to another, for his own harm (Locke 1988, 336–337)."

6.3 Reinterpreting Civil Disobedience as Disobedient Disclosure

My brief historical exegesis above establishes that – contrary to critics of its post-9/11 uses – executive prerogative fits into the theory of constitutional government derived from the authority of the people, in addition to aligning with the definition of civil disobedience. That said, however, a contemporary critics of prerogative, like Snowden, is concerned specifically with the *concealment* of extra-legal discretion, thus eliding public scrutiny and judgment. Obviously, public disclosure of such concealed uses for the people's judgment is necessary in order to meet Locke's requirements for justification. Nevertheless, this calls for a reinterpretation of the theory of civil disobedience. After all, the standard Rawlsian theory conceives of the justification of extra-legality by citizens in terms of addressing to the people about something they already know. Moreover, it conceives of such justification as attributing responsibility for this known injustice to the people themselves. It does not conceive of justification in light of disclosing some purported injustice, unknown to the public at large, and attributable to the executive power of government, as responsible party; neither does it express any popular anxieties about the potential for the executive power of government to turn tyrannical and rebel against the people.

Rawls indeed defines civil disobedience as a "mode of public address" that is "conscientious yet political act … guided and justified by political principles … regulat[ing] the constitution and social institutions generally" (1971, 364–365). To this extent, I interpret civil disobedience as a kind of *citizens' prerogative*: citizens exercise their own right of discretion to act, in a conscientious and principled way, outside the boundaries of law. Here, disobedience reflects a concern with the idea that "in one's considered opinion the principles of social cooperation among free and equal men are not being respected (Ibid, 364)." In more Lockean language, Rawlsian disobedients draw public attention to arrangements not all rational creatures could willingly consent to. Some such creatures experience disrespect for their fundamental freedom and equality, resulting in subordination for their harm. Rawlsian disobedients thus appeal to equal respect and non-subordination in the circumstance of the piecewise (Sabl 2001) distribution of basic constitutional rights and liberties, discriminating between a majority and minority of citizens. In this circumstance, the society practices justice – albeit in a piecewise manner – insofar as the rule of law fully respects the freedom and equality of the majority. Nevertheless, it does not practice justice inclusively by extending the ideals of equal respect and non-subordination to the minority.

In recent U.S. history, the key example for this is the disrespect shown for the freedom and equality of Black Americans in the 1950s, subordinated to the White majority, under racial segregation, or Jim Crow, laws. As rational creatures in the Lockean sense, Black Americans cannot be supposed to have willingly subordinated themselves to White Americans. Consequently, the piecewise distribution of rights and liberties between Black and White Americans was clearly a violation of the non-subordination principle, delegitimizing Jim Crow. Indeed, it was clearly such a violation insofar as disrespect for Black Americans was socially visible, a matter of common public knowledge. To this extent, it was quite different from the circumstance of injustice that concerns me in this article, whereby citizens disobediently disclose concealed uses of executive prerogative. After all, the non-subordination principle – according to Locke – invalidates prerogative *only* when the executive power acts tyrannically by rebelling against people, *as a whole*, taking away their liberties. To this extent, any such use – or, better, abuse – of prerogative is a 'wholesale' rather than a piecewise injustice. As a wholesale injustice, it affects all of the people indiscriminately, or without exception, subordinating all of them rather than upholding the rights of some but not others.

This difference between piecewise and wholesale injustice points to a significant disconnection between Rawlsian civil disobedience and disobedient disclosure concerning the attribution of responsibility for injustice. In the case of piecewise injustice, the people itself is collectively responsible for having created the injustice motivating the disobedients' action. As in the above example of Jim Crow or racial segregation laws, the injustice arises from past acts of their own legislative will (Markovits 2005), not any extra-legal discretionary acts by the executive. In the case of wholesale injustice, civil disobedience has to assign responsibility for the injustice to the executive. Indeed, the mode of disobedient public address for wholesale injustice cannot be supposed to consist in asking the Rawlsian question regarding piecewise injustice: Do you wish to have your past legislative decisions construed as violating the principles of justice for the constitutional order, or do you wish to reconsider? This is an inappropriate question, insofar as the purported injustice resulting from concealed uses of extra-legal discretion is not anything for which the people themselves bear responsibility in the same way that they are responsible for their self-legislative acts.

Consequently, disobedient disclosers should instead be seen as addressing the people with the Lockean question from the previous section: Has the executive made 'right use of' its power of prerogative, or has it misused this power in such a way that it has rebelled against those who originally constituted it for their mutual, public good? This overtly Lockean – as opposed to Rawlsian – question is more appropriate not only because it gets right the attribution of responsibility for the injustice purported by the disclosers. Nevertheless, it is also more appropriate because it avoids begging the justificatory question against the prerogative. Indeed, it avoids assuming that executive departures from popular legal mandate by post-9/11 governments are nothing but arbitrary exercises of executive power gone awry. Instead, it takes seriously the prerogative as possibly being a justifiable response to existential threats to the people. However, this means that disobedient disclosure should be understood as concerned with ensuring the normative legitimacy of the prerogative by exposing its concealed uses to public scrutiny and judgment. Such a concern with ensuring its legitimate use by exposing it to the people's considered judgment – or so I now contend – becomes the basis for both the definition and justification of disobedient disclosures.

Indeed, I define such disclosure as a recursive extra-legal discretionary act by citizens, addressing the people as a whole about the need to assess the legitimacy of extra-legal discretionary acts by the executive, when these have been deliberately concealed from public view and, as such, the possibility of popular judgment. Its justification, then, is to ensure the legitimacy and constitutionality of the prerogative by virtue of such disclosure resulting in the people's judgment of the executive. In summary, once reinterpreted this way, civilly disobedient disclosure does not invite the people to reconsider anything for which they are properly at fault. Nevertheless, it rather invites the people to consider whether by stepping outside established legal parameters the government has become a tyrant, or whether it is acting in a manner that is consistent with its proper end. Above all, my definition and justification avoids the false assumption made by some critics of prerogative, as noted earlier, that extra-legal discretion by the executive power of government is indefensible by appeal to the principles and ends of constitutional government. Disclosers have to acknowledge that it may be legitimate for post-9/11 governments to resort to extra-legal discretion, behind the backs of the people, as an expression of fidelity to the constitutional order.

6.4 Some Problems for the Reinterpretation

In the previous section, I highlighted the special recursive feature of disobedient disclosure, whereby citizens turn to extra-legal discretion in defense of core constitutional principles in order to invite the people to consider the legitimacy of the executive doing the same. Nevertheless, such recursivity in its definition and justification creates two closely related problems for disobedient disclosure. The first is that such disclosure potentially exposes the people, as public addressees, to existential risks not faced by Rawlsian civil disobedients concerned with piecewise inequalities. Indeed, the concealed uses of executive prerogative and their disclosure begs the justificatory question, absent acknowledgement of the potential for exposing the people to such risks. In Rawlsian civil disobedience, any risks accompanying the disobedient acts are strictly limited to the disobedients themselves. Rawlsian disobedients may expose themselves, for instance, to the risks of police brutality, but their addressees do not share these risks. Instead, the addressees have the luxury of reconsidering their complicity in the injustice of discrimination against a minority, while remaining personally secure with respect to their life, limb, and property.

As closely related to the first problem, the second problem is that disobedient disclosure could undermine what turn out to be necessary and legitimate efforts of the executive to preserve the people against genuine existential risks by resorting to secrecy and concealment. Acknowledging this is, again in the interest of not begging the question of justification. Here, the rationale for the executive keeping use of its power of prerogative concealed from public view is obviously to avoid alerting those who would do harm to the people about those efforts it is taking to preserve them. To be sure, disclosure does not necessarily expose the people to any increased risk. After all, the executive might be honestly mistaken about the level of risk posed by those who would do them harm, or it might be acting insincerely, exaggerating the threat to enhance its own powers. Nevertheless, the potential remains for disclosers to increase the peoples' exposure to risk by inviting them to deliberate whether the executive was justified in concealing its resort to extra-legality. Consequently, in light of the recursive reinterpretation of civil disobedience, these two closely related problems – exposing the people to existential risk, while undermining the executive's ability to protect them from such risk – lead to a potential self-contradiction in the act of disobedient disclosure.

Such potential for self-contradiction arises insofar as the purpose of the people constituting a government – in the Lockean terms presently under discussion – is to secure their self-preservation. Nevertheless, disclosers certainly appear to contradict such a purpose by preventing the executive from fulfilling the end for which the people originally constituted the government. To this extent, an objection is that, by contrast with Rawlsian civil disobedients, disobedient disclosers do not show proper *fidelity* to the constitutional order. If that is the case, however, then the reinterpretation from the previous section fails, and disobedient disclosure is not rightly be seen as any form of civil disobedience. Instead, it is as an affront to the ideal of a government constituted by the people for their self-preservation and mutual benefit. Indeed, on this analysis, the special recursive feature of disobedient disclosure disqualifies it as civil disobedience because extra-legality by the disclosers – exposing the extra-legality of the executive – does not take into account the end of self-preservation. How, then, might the objection that disobedient disclosure contradicts the end for which the people constituted a government be countered, thereby reclaiming the constitutional propriety of the recursive reinterpretation?

Perhaps the most obvious way to counter this objection is to deny that disclosers need either expose the people to risk or undermine the executive's efforts at securing popular self-preservation. This counter-move results in inconsistency, however, as long as the possibility is open that the executive may have been right to use its prerogative. Nonetheless, such a possibility of the executive being right about the danger facing the people surely points to the advisability of delaying disclosure. That is, points to the advisability of delay until the disclosers judge that the danger to the people has passed and, as such, disclosure would not expose them to any increased level of existential risk. To this extent, delay would create moral parity with Rawlsian civil disobedients in that disobedient disclosers would expose only themselves to risk – say, the risk of prosecution or retaliation by the executive – and not their public addressees. Nevertheless, even if such prudential delay avoids exposing the people to risks from which the executive is trying to protect them, it soon runs into an obvious difficulty of its own.

If, on the one hand, the executive has acted sincerely for the public good, and based on sound intelligence, then it will presumably voluntarily self-disclose once the danger has passed and disclosure poses no heightened risk to the people. In doing so, it would thereby subject itself to retrospective, or ex post facto, public scrutiny and judgment. Indeed, as long as its motives are pure – fulfilling the end of popular self-preservation – then the executive has no reason not to self-disclose. Not, at any rate, insofar as it can be confident that the people will find cause to judge in its favor. Nevertheless, such voluntary self-disclosure by the executive would also appear to make any resort to delayed disobedient disclosure quite redundant. After all, if that were the case, then there would be nothing for citizens to disclose disobediently. Nevertheless, if, on the other hand, the executive did not act sincerely for the public good on sound intelligence, then it will presumably lack voluntarily self-disclose as a motivation. Instead, it will likelier than not want to keep its unjustifiable use of prerogative permanently concealed from public view and scrutiny, fearing the consequences of an adverse public reaction and outcry. To this extent, however, far from being redundant disobedient disclosure would become relevant and appropriate, when it becomes evident to citizens with knowledge of what the executive is doing that the latter is indeed unwilling to self-disclose for such unacceptable reasons.

But, that said, it might just as well be said that it would also be relevant and appropriate for such citizens to disclose what they know much sooner. After all, the decision to delay disclosure would have unnecessarily condemned the people to live for a time with the suspension of their fundamental rights and liberties. Disclosing sooner the executive's departure from legal mandate and constitutional principle might well have brought to light its descent into mere arbitrariness and tyranny by virtue of public scrutiny. Indeed, such 'timely' disobedient disclosure could have resulted earlier in a negative popular judgment, contesting the executive who is in rebellion against the people and acting for their harm. That way, the people might have reclaimed their lost rights and liberties a lot more quickly than if those with relevant information had opted for delay. Nevertheless, following this line of reasoning, timely disclosure would be justifiable even if those with information about executive extra-legality believe that the executive is acting in good conscience and is willing to self-disclose, at an appropriate future time. Citizens with knowledge of the executive's concealed use of prerogative may hold a mistaken belief in its sincerity, in which case the people will likewise suffer an unnecessary loss of rights and liberties, denied the opportunity to reach their own judgment in the full light of publicity.

Where does this present analysis now leave us, if delayed disclosure fails to answer the objection that disclosure potentially contradicts the ends for government? I contend it points to a classical dilemma for disobedient disclosers in which they are 'damned if they do and damned if they don't.' On the one hand, if citizens opt to disclose in a timely fashion, they could undermine the legitimate efforts of the executive – who acts in good conscience, etc. – to preserve the people. On the other hand, if they delay disclosure, then they take from the people the opportunity to make an appropriately principled judgment of their own regarding the executive's extra-legal activities. Does this dilemma mean that the objection remains standing, calling for rejection of the recursive reinterpretation of civil disobedience? I argue next that this is not so, and that the notion of disclosers resorting to extra-legal discretion, so as to invite reconsideration of the executive doing the same, can be reclaimed.

6.5 Reclaiming the Recursive Reinterpretation

My argument for reclaiming the recursive reinterpretation now depends on creating a much closer conceptual alignment of extra-legal discretion by citizens with Locke's concept of executive prerogative than with the standard Rawlsian model of civil disobedience. Indeed, I want to argue that disobedient disclosure aligns with prerogative insofar as the dilemma faced by the disclosers places them in much the same justificatory situation as the executive who resorts to concealed forms of extra-legal discretion for the public good. After all, such an executive is faced with an inescapable 'damned if you do, damned if you don't' dilemma of its own. On the one hand, if the executive acts on what it believes to be good intelligence in order to preserve the people, then it may unnecessarily suspend those rights and liberties falling under the non-subordination principle in a wholesale fashion. Let us say, the suspension turns out to have been an honest mistake based on what emerges as faulty intelligence, in light of public scrutiny, following disclosure of one kind or another. But, on the other hand, if it fails to exercise its prerogative in the interest of maintaining strict compliance with non-subordination, at all times, including those times it believes there is genuine existential risk to the people, then it may well undermine popular self-preservation. Let us say, some significant part of the people suffers loss of life or limb, along with the destruction of property where this may include not only private but also public property, such as vital public infrastructure, affecting untold numbers of lives.

Here, the executive faces having to make a judgment in one way or the other. Nevertheless, either way, it has to 'balance,' or rather assign differential weights, to competing principles of constitutional order. If it exercises its prerogative, then it will assign a greater weight to popular self-preservation than to non-subordination. As for disobedient disclosers, they are in essentially the same justificatory situation as the executive contemplating resort to prerogative. That is, they are in the same situation of having to balance the competing principles of self-preservation and non-subordination. The only substantive difference is that they contemplate performing a contrary act of balancing, assigning a greater weight to non-subordination than to self-preservation. Of course, the notion of balancing is notoriously difficult (see, for instance, Kleinerman 2007; Hayden 2005; Waldron 2003). But most, if not all (Neocleous 2007), commentators on post-9/11 uses of executive prerogative do acknowledge the necessity and legitimacy of striking some appropriate balance of competing principles of self-preservation and non-subordination, or – in somewhat different but related language – 'security and liberty.' Can, though, the same necessity and legitimacy assigned to discretionary acts by the executive be assigned to those discretionary acts of disobedient disclosers to the extent neither can properly avoid making an agonistic judgment about the balancing of these principles?

This is to ask if it is objectively justifiable for disobedient citizens to make an *executive judgment of their own* about what is and is not necessary for the people's self-preservation, as implied by their particular act of balancing competing principles. Clearly, the executive power of government is justified in making judgments of this kind because the people have licensed or authorized it to do so by constituting a government whose end is to ensure their collective self-preservation. However, what about the disclosers? Here, an objection is that the people have not authorized them, as citizens possessing information about the executive's concealed use of prerogative, to exercise such a power to assess existential risks to life, limb, and property. To this extent, disclosers have overstepped the bounds of legitimate disobedience, as extra-legal discretion exercised by citizens rather than the officials of the constitutional state. It is one thing for disobedients to address the people about piecewise injustices or, for that matter, to disclose clear acts of executive malfeasance, when this facilitates reform without exposing the people to existential risks. Nevertheless, it is quite another to say that they can legitimately disclose executive acts that are not clearly done for the harm of the people and, in doing so, potentially expose them to such risks.

Is there, then, a reason to say that it is properly within the remit of citizens to make judgments, assigning differential weights to the principles of self-preservation and non-subordination? I contend the answer to this question is yes, and for the reason already identified in my brief historical exegesis of Locke's constitutionalism. There, I stressed not only that the people authorize prerogative by transferring their own executive power, under the law of nature, to the government they constitute, but also that such a power is not surrendered as much as it is held in reserve. In other words, their original executive power to interpret the law of nature, and make judgments about fidelity to basic principles, is not something that citizens ever give up when they constitute a government, and authorize it to make painful and contestable judgments about balancing fundamental principles. For citizens to give up their right and duty to 'do the same' as the executive should, they find good reasons to question its judgment to repudiate the ideal of constitutionalism. Consequently, the principles of constitutional order equally bind executive and citizens in such a way that they cannot avoid making judgments about how to balance and assign the relative weights of such principles.

Indeed, when conflicts of such principles arise, neither can walk away from the moral obligation to make a judgment, however painful and contestable. But, if this is correct, then the recursive redefinition of disobedient disclosure is indeed reclaimed through the alignment of both kinds of resort to extra-legality by executive and disobedient disclosers to the extent that both make – albeit contradictory – judgments about balancing conflicting principles for the public good. Does it matter that the judgments variously made by executive and citizens, balancing self-preservation and non-subordination, come into conflict with one another? At this point, I believe the answer to that question is rather clearly no. That they come into conflict is uninteresting from the justificatory standpoint. Both judgments are justified to the extent that they appeal to fundamental constitutional principles, regardless of their differential justificatory weights. In the final analysis, the differential weights of judgments reached by executive and disclosers fall within the boundaries of legitimacy and, as such, *loyal disagreement* for the constitutional order. That is, they fall within these boundaries, granting that this order is unable to guarantee that fidelity to its fundamental principles may always be realized through strict compliance with the law.

Two further consequences follow from my claim that the conflicting judgments of executive and disclosers fall within the boundaries of loyal disagreement. On the one hand, it precludes any appeal to transparency as a human right (Birkinshaw 2006). On the other hand, it requires leniency for executive and disclosers by appeal to the criterion of personal conscience or sincerity.

6.6 Transparency and Leniency

Transparency aims to enable "the public to gain information about the operations of and structures of a given entity (Etzioni 2010, 389)," such as a particular branch or agency of government. As such, it intuitively aligns with disclosure, so much so that it is "often considered synonymous … with disclosure" (Ibid). It is, then, no surprise that Julian Assange, the founder of the WikiLeaks organization, has claimed transparency is a human right (Fenster 2012). Hence, as a human right "to know, to speak, and to communicate information" (Ibid, 773), transparency purportedly underwrites disobedient disclosure, in the cases of WikiLeaks releasing the "War Logs," compiling secret US diplomatic cables regarding the Afghanistan, or the video "Collateral Damage," documenting a US war crime in Iraq that had been kept from the public. Assange claims that "if we maximize the reliable, verified information about how the world is working, then we start to produce more sophisticated and intelligent structures that respond to the abuses in society and also the opportunities there may be in society" (see interview with Assange in Harrell 2010).

In this respect, Assange sees transparency as expressing an ideal of scientific journalism, allowing "you to read a news story, then click online to see the original document it is based on. That way you can judge for yourself: Is the story true? Did the journalist report it accurately? (Assange 2010). Consequently, the disclosure of secret government documents provides "scientific, true data to an inquiring public that will act on the truth as it is presented (Ibid). Here, the redaction of information to avoid foreseeable risks of harms to persons mentioned in the disclosed documents is only limit on disobedient disclosure. Overall, as an expression of scientific journalism, transparency is continuous with established human rights, such as freedom of speech along with access to justice and the rule of law. It is also continuous with the ideal of freedom of information, which falls "within the framework of internationally agreed concepts of human rights" (Birkinshaw 2006, 47). Moreover, from a Rawlsian standpoint in *Law of Peoples* (2001), transparency falls within these boundaries, as long as it fits into the special class of urgent rights concerned with the preservation of life and limb, along with access to the rule of law.

It is unclear that WikiLeaks' release of the War Logs meets this standard, insofar as it amounted to a generalized 'data dump' (subject to prudential redactions) that did not expose any particular injustice at this level of existential urgency. Nevertheless, the standard is met in the case of the Collateral Damage video and Snowden's disclosure of the NSA's mass collection of US citizens' metadata. On the one hand, the standard is met because the disobedient disclosure exposed a War Crime, involving the loss of innocent non-combatant lives. On the other hand, it is met because the disclosure exposed violations of civil rights defining the moral character of the people of a constitutional state. Here, transparency as an urgent human right makes sense in the first of the latter two cases. Concealing a war crime is not an act of executive prerogative as conceived by Locke. It is not necessary to fulfil any of the proper ends of government. On the contrary, it amounts to an arbitrary use of governmental power. Nevertheless, transparency as an urgent human right has no justificatory value for resolving the second case. There is clearly no valid justification that could be given, in light of the ends of government, for machine gunning journalists and children from a US Army attack helicopter. There is, however, a case that could be made – albeit controversially – for the mass collection of US citizens' meta-data with the sincere intention not of violating civil rights, but rather preserving their life and limb given the prospect of future terrorist attacks.

Of course, Snowden and his supporters could argue – just as controversially – that the *more urgent* threat is to the continued existence or preservation of a people, as defined by its commitments to such rights. But that is precisely the reason why transparency fails to resolve the dilemma of executive and citizens making contradictory justifiable claims about the proper balancing of self-preservation and non-subordination. Indeed, it arbitrarily affirms one justifiable claim at the expense of another, failing to grasp the full complexity of political life, as sometimes entailing contradictory but equally justifiable claims grounded in fundamental principles. Consequently, a different approach is needed, one taking into account the ambivalence of justifiable claim making. This points not to a human right to government transparency, but rather leniency for disobedient acts with equally valid but contradictory claims to justifiability. Here, leniency for executive and citizens is a mandate of reasonableness among decent peoples, responding to the irreducible complexity of politics.

I have already argued that it is uninteresting from a justificatory point of view that the judgements of executive and citizens conflict with one another. Nevertheless, such conflicts are interesting from the point of view of justifiable penalizations. Here, the issue is instead the just punishment of executive and disclosers, exceeding the mandates of the law based on different claims to protect the rights and interests of the people. Indeed, a key part of the justification for civil disobedience is the willingness to accept the legal consequences of disobedience. This is a requirement of expressing fidelity to the principle of the rule of law, distinguishing the disobedient from revolutionary or anarchist (Rawls 1971). By contrast, discussions of executive prerogative rarely, if ever, engage the question of just penalization, even though an executive resorting to prerogative is a disobedient in the terms laid out earlier in this chapter. This suggests an important dis-analogy between executive prerogative and civil disobedience, despite those similarities I have stressed so far. Hence, even though prerogative is justified in terms of constitutional fidelity, an executive resorting to prerogative, and claiming justification in doing so by appeal to a sincere belief that extra-legality is necessary to preserve the public good, need not express such constitutional fidelity in terms of a willingness to accept legal consequences.

Nevertheless, the critic of executive prerogative might well ask why this dis-analogy should hold. If extra-legality justified in term of constitutional commitments requires the willingness to accept penalties in the case of civil disobedience, then the same should hold for executive officers of the state. After all, both executive and disobedient citizen claim the same ground of justification in constitutional fidelity. The dis-analogy of executive and citizens regarding the expectation of a willingness to accepting legal consequences is due, in part, to Locke's discussion of executive prerogative, which presupposes its legitimacy as necessary to fulfil the end of preserving life, limb, and property. Here, Locke's example of pulling down a burning house to prevent others from catching fire is uncontroversial by comparison with post-911 examples of executive prerogative, such as the PRISM program, widely viewed by its critics as violating basic civil liberties of citizens. In the post-911 cases, civil libertarian critics may justifiably call for the prosecution of government officials who violate constitutional rights. Indeed, such calls are pragmatically defensible on the ground that they are necessary to deter future civil liberties violations and ensure the preservation of constitutional rule, as opposed to arbitrary, tyrannical rule. Nevertheless, defenders of prerogative may rightly object that harsh prosecution and punishment is counterproductive to the proper ends of constitutional government because it may disincentivize officials from acting on their conscience for the public good, in the event of future existential threats to the people. That said, however, recognizing the necessity and legitimacy of prerogative does not rule out prosecution and penalization for officials.

Indeed, the argument for willingness to accept penalties in the context of civil disobedience also applies to executive prerogative, subject to a number of important caveats. Civil disobedients need to reassure the public whom they address that they are not revolutionaries and anarchists in order to establish a basis of credibility and trust. In other words, the addressees must be able to believe that the disobedients are sincere in wanting to uphold the fundamental principles of the rule of law, if they are to take seriously their own moral obligation to reconsider its present defects. Without such trust, they are likelier than not motivated to respond defensively, fearing that disobedience jeopardizes even the piecewise order of justice. By contrast, in the case of secretive uses of executive prerogative, there are no public addressees. Nevertheless, executive officers resorting to such uses of prerogative are always aware of the potential for the disobedient disclosure of their discretionary judgements to exceed the mandates of law for the public good. They know that in the event of such disclosure citizens may interpret their actions as a major breach of public trust, undermining belief in the institutions of constitutional government expressing the moral character of the people. The people may thus interpret secretive uses of executive prerogative as an existential assault by a would-be tyrant.

Under this circumstance of such high potential to undermine public trust in constitutionalism, an executive ought to be willing to accept legal consequences as an expression of constitutional fidelity.[1]

[1] Here I appeal only to the case in which the executive's secretive use of prerogative is disobediently disclosed. Nevertheless, an executive also ought to voluntarily self-disclose to the people past the point of urgency or immediate public danger. This follows as a requirement of taking seriously the publicity standard of decency in the *Law of Peoples* (2001). Indeed, any justification for secrecy no longer holds once that point is passed, regardless of the legal and political consequences for the executive.

Nevertheless, subject to the same requirement to express fidelity by accepting penalties, an executive also ought to enjoy the same kind of special consideration in sentencing enjoyed by civilly disobedient citizens. Indeed, regarding civil disobedience, the sincerity of the disobedients' belief that the protection of fundamental principles of justice is at stake, along with their ability to support this belief with public reasons appealing to such principles, entitles them to leniency in sentencing, if not outright amnesty (Brownlee 2008; also see Dworkin 1968). Here, leniency itself is properly a requirement of decency and reasonableness for peoples. It is unreasonable for peoples to refuse uptake and reconsideration in light of public reasons offered in terms of fundamental principles of justice. Of course, this does not mean that the outcomes of deliberation over these reasons will always be what the disobedients would want. After all, the deliberative outcome might be a contestable judgment to the effect that they have somehow misunderstood the situation in question as one of fundamental injustice, contrary to what they believe in all sincerity while publicly exposing themselves to risk of penalties. Nevertheless, the sincerity of this belief, as supported by defensible public reasons, ought to be taken into consideration in sentencing. Not to do so would show disrespect for the moral character of a people committed to those principles to which the disobedients have demonstrated their fidelity by accepting the risk of legal consequences. Failure to show leniency would be tantamount to denying the special value of constitutional patriotism as embodying the fundamental commitments defining the people's moral character.

It is one thing to disagree with the reasons of a constitutional patriot like Snowden, but it is quite another to treat such a patriot as no different from a mere criminal or a traitor. But the same holds for officials of the executive power, supposing they demonstrate an equal fidelity to constitutional principles by accepting equal risks of public judgment and penalization. This, however, leaves open the question of extending the present analysis of executive prerogative and disobedient disclosure to traditional-hierarchical societies. Can the analysis be put into a truly global perspective through such an extension?

6.7 Extending the Analysis to Traditional-Hierarchical Societies

The justification for disobedience depends on having public reasons capable of defeating the prima facie duty of officials and citizens alike to stay within the boundaries of the law. Up to this point, my discussion has presupposed the context of a modern liberal state. Nevertheless, liberal constitutionalism need not be the only source of public reasons defeating the duty to obey. Indeed, I have argued in the preceding chapters that the urgency and decency standards of the *Law of Peoples* (2001) function as moral considerations capable of defeating this duty. Indeed, the urgent need to preserve the people, as many as can be, is surely also an end of government for the officials of traditional-hierarchical societies, bound by a common good conception of justice. To this extent, the officials of such societies may also claim the right of prerogative, exercising their sincere and conscientious belief that going beyond the mandates of law is sometimes necessary for the public good of a hierarchically ordered people. This not only applies in Locke's uncontroversial case of pulling down the burning building to prevent any further spread of fire, but also the controversial post-911 case of secretly surveilling citizens in the interest of collecting information that might prevent a terrorist attack. After all, the officials of traditional-hierarchical societies have an equal interest as their counterparts in liberal-democratic societies in preserving their citizens against existential threats posed by international terrorism.

Is there, however, an equivalent justification for the disobedient disclosure of secret government surveillance programs by the citizens of traditional-hierarchical societies? An objection to this possibility could be that the common good conception for such a society does not offer constitutional safeguards against government intrusions into citizens' private lives, such as the US Fourth Amendment. But still publicity and the rule of law is a central feature of the decency commitment of all peoples. A hierarchically ordered society have legitimate interests in maintaining a kind of surveillance that should not be tolerated in a liberal-democracy, organized on the basis of an equal distribution of civil and political rights. For instance, the ruling elite of a traditional-hierarchical people might legitimately claim an interest in monitoring conformity with an inegalitarian, differential distribution of rights and duties, based on group memberships. Indeed, it might justifiably see this kind of monitoring as demanded by its obligation to maintain the common good conception of justice, defining the moral character of such a people. Nevertheless, surveillance in the interest of maintaining the common good conception of justice would presumably be public knowledge and publicly justified in light of this conception.

The situation is quite different supposing that surveillance is conducted secretively, even though it could be justified along the same lines as necessary to preserve the people as defined by its distinctive moral character. That said, however, does it also follow that the citizens of a traditional-hierarchical society have a right to disobedient disclosure? I have already argued that the citizens of such a society have a moral right to disobey, based not on claims to justice grounded in respect for equal civil and political rights, but rather the various considerations of decency, which include the publicity of decisions taken by their ruling elites. To this extent, those with access to informative kept secret may justifiably disclose what they know by appeal to the publicity standard of decency, provided they sincerely believe this exposes some other violation of decency. This could be the exposure of a war crime the ruling elite is trying to conceal, analogous to the case of the Collateral Damage video released by WikiLeaks. Alternatively, it could be that disclosers reveal evidence that the secretive actions of the elite are not sincerely motivated by the public good. For example, the elite is acting tyrannically by surveilling legitimate dissenters with the intention of violating rights to which they are entitled as members of particular groups in the stratified social order. In other words, disclosers could not make the kind of appeal that Snowden made to violations of privacy rights, under the US constitution. Nevertheless, they could still make sundry appeals to violations of global decency standards, as freestanding of liberal-democratic constitutionalism.

Decency functions, again, as the basis of a global public discourse of peoples and cosmopolitan citizens. Indeed, executives resorting to secretive uses of prerogative are cosmopolitan citizens. An immediate objection to this designation for is that their actions are state-centric to the extent they act only to preserve the life and moral character of the particular people they serve. Nevertheless, in acting to preserve this one people, they also act to preserve one vital part of the international community of decent peoples. Moreover, they promote what I called, in Chap. 1, moderate cosmopolitanism. This is concerned with upholding the normative priority of decent states and peoples, as basis for a stable and robust international order of human rights. As cosmopolitan citizens, however, executives are subject to the publicity requirement of decency that they should be willing to face legal consequences at some appropriate time.

Disobedient disclosers of government secrets are also cosmopolitan citizens, within the paradigm of moderate cosmopolitanism. Snowden was a US citizen disclosing US government secrets, but he addressed the international community of peoples, as well as the US people, through his various disclosures. As for WikiLeaks, this is clearly a multinational coalition of disobedient cosmopolitan citizens, intending their disclosures to be global in scope. Such a coalition need not be restricted to citizens from constitutional liberal-democracies. Indeed, the decency criteria of *Law of Peoples* underwrites disobedient cosmopolitan citizens from traditional hierarchical societies participating in WikiLeaks disclosures. They could participate by appealing to reasons grounded in their common good conception of justice, but consistent with international decency requirements shared with their coalition peers from liberal-democracies.

Nevertheless, such an international coalition would be restricted normatively in its ability to offer reasons grounded in equal civil and political rights to the people of a traditional-hierarchical society, as justification for disclosing secretive uses of prerogative by the ruling elite of that society. This restriction on legitimate reason-giving to those reasons grounded in internationally shared decency standards would be a requirement of respect for the autonomy of peoples and their capacities to undertake reform through internal dissent (Beitz 2011; Rawls 2001). Granting a restriction of legitimate reason-giving to shared decency standards rather civil and political equality, the justification of contradictory and competing claim to justifiable disobedience is extended to all decent societies. As such, it placed in a genuinely global perspective, despite the analysis having been originally motivated through a discussion of fidelity to liberal constitutionalism.

6.8 Conclusion

In this chapter, I have taken seriously the idea that constitutionalism is consistent with resort to extra-legality. This idea may be familiar enough in the case of Rawlsian civil disobedience. But I have focused my discussion differently. In particular, I have focused on the justifiability of such resort in the case of concealed uses of Lockean prerogative by the executive power of government and its disobedient disclosure by citizens possessing knowledge of what the former is doing behind the backs of the people. Indeed, taking seriously the compatibility of extra-legal discretion with the constitutional rule of law, I have argued that both concealed use of prerogative and its disobedient disclosure can be justified. Prerogative can be justified for the reason already identified by Locke: not all contingencies can be anticipated in law and so some discretionary judgment is necessary in order for the executive to fulfill the end of self-preservation for which government was constituted by the people. If the necessity of prerogative is accepted for this reason, then extra-legal discretion by the executive power cannot simply be dismissed as tyrannical, government rebellion against the people.

As for disobedient disclosure, this can be justified, again, for the reason already identified by Locke; the legitimacy of prerogative is subject to contestation and popular judgment. This indeed is the condition for non-subordination and non-tyranny. But disclosure has the potential to pit the goal of non-subordination against that of self-preservation, so that disclosure operates at cross-purposes with prerogative. That does not, however, entail the incoherence of saying that both may be justifiable. Not, at any rate, as long as both may appeal to an idea of needing to balance competing principles of constitutional order. This appeal to balancing acknowledges that conflicts of principles may sometimes arise, especially from emergency situations that could not be unanticipated by law, and that unavoidable, agonistic judgments simply have to be made. Although they might well differ across the perspectives of executive and disclosers, judgments about balancing, or weighing differentially, the principles of non-subordination and self-preservation, when they compete, remain sincere expressions of constitutional fidelity.

This analysis led me to dismiss the idea that transparency is an urgent human right on the ground that it arbitrarily validates one justifiable claim to extra-legality over another. However, I argued that leniency for executive and disclosers alike is a requirement of the reasonableness and decency of peoples. Grounding justification in these moral characteristics of all decent peoples. I argued finally for extending the analysis from liberal constitutionalism to the international community of peoples generally, including hierarchically ordered peoples whose fidelity is to a non-egalitarian common good conception of justice. Subject to caveats, my analysis thus establishes the possibility of a global perspective on the secretive uses of executive prerogative and disobedient disclosure. In this respect, it takes seriously the moderate cosmopolitan proposition that liberal-democracy does not hold a global monopoly on claims to decency and justice. Indeed, consistent with my overall goals for this book, the present chapter grounds controversial and contestable claims to the justifiability of discretionary extra-legality for the public good in a global public discourse of decency.

References

Assange, Julian. 2010. Editorial. The Australian, December 7.

Beitz, Charles. 2011. *The Idea of Human Rights*. Oxford: Oxford University Press.

Birkinshaw, Patrick. 2006. Transparency as a Human Right. In *Transparency: The Key to Better Governance?* ed. Christopher Hood and David Heald, 47–57. Oxford: Oxford University Press.

Bouville, Mathieu. 2008. Whistleblowing and Morality. *Journal of Business Ethics* 81(3): 579–585.

Brownlee, Kimberley. 2008. Penalizing Civil Disobedience. *Ethics* 118:4, 711–716.

Brownlee, Kimberlee. 2012. *Conscience and Conviction: The Case for Civil Disobedience*. Oxford: Oxford University Press.

Delmas, Candace. 2015. The Ethics of Government Whistleblowing. *Social Theory and Practice* 41(1): 77–105.
Dworkin, Ronald. 1968. Editorial. New York Review of Books, June 6.
Etzioni, Amitai. 2010. Is Transparency the Best Disinfectant? *Journal of Political Philosophy* 18(4): 389–404.
Fatovic, Clement. 2001. Constitutionalism and Contingency: Locke's Theory of Prerogative. *History of Political Thought* 25(2): 276–297.
Fenster, Mark. 2012. Disclosure's Effects: WikiLeaks and Transparency. *Iowa Law Review* 97(3): 753–807.
Greenwald, Glenn. 2014. *No Place to Hide: Edward Snowden, the NSA, and the US Surveillance State*. Northampton: Metropolitan Books.
Harrel, Eben. 2010. *Defending the Leaks: Q and A with Wikileak's Jullian Assange*. Time, July 27.
Hayden, Michael. 2005. Balancing Security and Liberty: The Challenge of Sharing Foreign Intelligence Signals. *Notre Dame Journal of Law Ethics and Public Policy* 19(1): 247–260.
Hood, Christopher, and David Heald, eds. 2006. *Transparency: The Key to Better Governance?* Oxford: Oxford University Press.
Kleinerman, Benjamin. 2007. Review Essay/9/11, the Liberty/Security Balance, and the Separation of Powers. *Criminal Justice Ethics* 26(1): 59–66.
Locke, John. 1988. *Two Treatises of Government*, Peter Laslett ed. Cambridge: Cambridge University Press.
Lovell, James. 2009. *Crimes of Dissent: Civil Disobedience, Criminal Justice and the Politics of Conscience*. New York: New York University Press.
Mattie, Sean. 2005. Prerogative and the Rule of Law in John Locke and the Lincoln Presidency. *Review of Politics* 67(1): 77–111.
Markovits, Daniel. 2005. Democratic Disobedience. *Yale Law Journal* 114: 198–948.
Muller, Jan-Werner. 2007. *Constitutional Patriotism*. Princeton: Princeton University Press.
Neocleous, Mark. 2007. Security, Liberty and the Myth of Balance: Towards a Critique of Security Politics. *Contemporary Political Theory* 6(2): 131–149.
Rawls, John. 1971. *A Theory of Justice*. Cambridge, MA: Harvard University Press.
Rawls, John. 2001. *The Law of Peoples*. Cambridge, MA: Harvard University Press.
Rehfeld, Andrew. 2008. Jephthah, the Hebrew Bible, and John Locke's 'Second Treatise of Government'. *Hebraic Political Studies* 3(1): 60–93.
Sabl, Andrew. 2001. Looking Forward to Justice: Rawlsian Civil Disobedience and Its Non-Rawlsian Lessons. *Journal of Political Philosophy* 9(3): 307–330.
Sager, R. 2013. *Secrets and Leaks: The Dilemma of State Secrecy*. Princeton: Princeton University Press.
Scheuerman, William. 2014. *Promises and Agreements: Philosophical Essays*. Oxford: Oxford University Press.
Smith, William. 2013. *Civil Disobedience and Deliberative Democracy*. New York: Routledge.
Waldron, Jeremy. 2003. Security and Liberty: The Image of Balance. *Journal of Political Philosophy* 11(2): 191–210.
Welchman, Jennifer. 2001. Is Ecosabotage Civil Disobedience? *Philosophy and Geography* 4(1): 97–107.

Chapter 7
Disobedience as an Expression of Global Solidarity and Redefining Disobedience in a Global Perspective

Abstract The three preceding cases of civil disobedience in a global perspective are expressions of global solidarity. Besides the addition of a human right to be a political participant, wherever you are, to the minimalist list of human rights in *Law of Peoples*, such disobedience does not otherwise point to any particular changes or reforms of law and policy. Its function is highlighting the piecewise just and unfair terms of global cooperation and motivating reconsideration by decent peoples that could lead to different kinds of policy outcomes based on the resulting processes of global public communication and deliberation. To this extent, the global civil disobedience practice of diverse cosmopolitan citizens express global solidarity with the undocumented and the global poor. Likewise, executives and disclosers express solidarity with decent peoples whom they see as facing different kinds of existential threats qua decent peoples. They do so in that disobedient cosmopolitan citizens adopt a perspective of concern for the most vulnerable in the system of merely piecewise just or unfair global cooperation. Indeed, this perspective of concern expresses a global solidarity relation. I then build on the discussion of diverse global civil disobedience practices as expressing global solidarity relations by offering an analytical redefinition of civil disobedience in a global perspective. This redefinition synthesizes the various claims of the preceding chapters regarding my extension of Rawls' state-centered definition and justification of civil disobedience in *Theory* to the *Law of Peoples*. It also identifies global solidarity as the principal aim of such an extension of justifiable civil disobedience to the global arena.

7.1 Introduction

The distinguishing feature of solidarity is that it is, above all, a *membership* concept. Nevertheless, the category of membership to which theorists of solidarity most frequently appeal is that of co-national citizenship. As such,

M. Allen, *Civil Disobedience in Global Perspective*,
Studies in Global Justice 16, DOI 10.1007/978-94-024-1164-5_7

solidarity is about a co-national 'we.' This 'we,' however, may be conceived as having feelings of empathy and acknowledging duties of universal humanitarian justice towards non-members – or "them" as distant others from other countries – without ever including the latter in 'our' exclusive solidaristic community of citizens (Nagel 2005; Miller 2012). This is true. Nevertheless, as I shall argue, this is a particularly narrow reading of solidarity. Indeed, the concept of solidarity may encompass many different forms of membership besides national citizenship. In particular, it properly applies to an international community of peoples as constituting an interconnected global system of terms and relations of cooperation. Consequently, I appeal to the idea of community in a broad sense of interdependency and cooperative relations transcending borders. In other words, I appeal the global 'we' of the international community of all decent peoples.

Here, all persons and peoples are members of the universal 'we' of this community. Indeed, all are properly the subjects of international concern (Beitz 2011), as owed respect for their shared human rights and autonomy. Nevertheless, solidarity of respect for human rights and the autonomy of peoples is hardly a reality in the condition of merely piecewise global justice and unfair terms of international cooperation. Consequently, I argue that the civilly disobedient calls of cosmopolitan citizens to reconsider the merely piecewise distribution of rights and opportunities to participate effectively in shaping the global terms of cooperation are inherently solidaristic acts. Such calls are solidaristic in the sense that those responsible for ensuring decency regarding such participation demonstrate an appropriate concern for the globally marginalized, impoverished, and so on, to ensure fair cooperative relations.

In this respect, global solidarity is an expression of international concern for diverse vulnerable others across the world, along with a commitment to eliminate vulnerability in cooperation, by those in a position of comparative security and power. Indeed, the 'assisted disobedience' (Brownlee 2012) by citizens on behalf of the undocumented as discussed in Chap. 3, and the disobedient acts of coalitions of cosmopolitan citizens as discussed in Chap. 5, are both expressions of solidarity relations in this sense. As for the relations of decent peoples to disobedient disclosers, these are likewise solidaristic relations to the extent that disclosers are highly vulnerable to retaliation from the national security state. That said, however, it is also the case that state officials resorting to secretive uses of prerogative are rendered vulnerable to public approbation – along with the possible loss of reputation and career, if not international prosecution – following disobedient disclosures. These vulnerabilities are clearly of a different order from the vulnerabilities of the undocumented and the global poor. Nevertheless, they are genuine vulnerabilities in cooperation that should be matters of international concern, given that both kinds of conscientious extra-legality are justifiable according to the international decency standard.

Solidarity relations in the latter case are also considerably broader in scope and relevance. Indeed, executives resorting to prerogative powers in undertaking secretive surveillance programs might well claim to be in solidarity with the potential victims of international terrorism. That is, they might claim to be in solidarity with all those vulnerable to future terrorist attacks. Similarly, disclosers might claim to be in solidarity with all those vulnerable to state surveillance and its potential misuse. Moreover, solidarity through disobedient acts of one kind or another is even an expression of solidarity in the sense that the disobedients expose themselves to vulnerabilities of prosecution. In this respect, the willingness of disobedients to run and indeed accept the risks of prosecution is not merely an expression of fidelity to the principle of the rule of law, but also an expression of the willingness to share in the risks of vulnerability to a disorder system of cooperation. In a disordered system, disobedients expose themselves to risk by 'doing the right thing,' highlighting and contesting piecewise justice and unfairness. Finally, recognition by decent peoples of an obligation to show leniency to executives and disclosers maintains solidarity between all those equally committed to decency, but otherwise divided by conflicting interpretations of its prescriptions.

In what follows, I first consider the concepts of solidarity and *global* solidarity in some more detail. I argue that the goal of diverse global civil disobedience practices is to create an *international solidaristic community*, guaranteeing effective access to the rule of law and its protections for all persons and peoples. In other words, the goal is to create global solidarity relations of non-domination for persons and peoples alike. I then proceed to an analytic redefinition of civil disobedience in a global perspective. Indeed, this redefinition builds on the insights of the previous chapters, while stressing global solidarity as the principal aim of such disobedience.

7.2 A Global Civil Disobedience Practice and Global Solidarity

In the above redefinition and in my three case studies I did not tie civil disobedience to any particular reforms of domestic or international law or policy concerning border controls, amnesty for the undocumented, global wealth redistributions prescribed by a global difference principle or global recourse dividend, and so on. Like civil disobedience, solidarity is fundamental tied to the goal of achieving a stable and inclusive social order according to principles of justice. Indeed, the idea of solidarity plays a vital role in the political philosophy literature by providing an account of how a stable and cohesive political community is forged (Rehg 1997; Harvey 2007; Lenard et al. 2010; Kolers 2012; Krishnamurthy 2013). That is, it provides an account of political community among diverse human populations with different needs, interests, ideological commitments and identities. For most political theorists, however, solidarity is not simply about *proximity* of relations. Solidarity relations may be proximity relations, as in the case of the undocumented. Nevertheless, they can also extend to distant others with whom those in solidarity never personally encounter, as in the case of global economic inequities.

In this regard, solidarity is sometimes defined in terms of culturally specific ideas of the good life, in all its many aspects and dimensions, among national citizens (Sandel 1997); only then, are citizens willing to make those sacrifices that *justice* demands of them for their co-nationals, whom they have never personally met. Nevertheless, this shared common good conception of solidarity has been criticized on the ground that it does not take into account the pluralism of commitments and values in any modern large-scale national political community (Krishnamurthy 2013). Moreover, as tied to the nation state, such a conception of solidarity has been further criticized for failing to provide an account of solidarity relations with non-nationals (Lenard et al. 2010; Straehle 2010). The first of these two criticisms is less than compelling. Indeed, I define solidarity more narrowly in political terms as a concern for guaranteeing effective access to the rule of law and appropriate political participation rights. On this alternative definition, concern for cultural pluralism is not central to solidarity, as along as diverse conceptions of the good life are compatible with the rule of law and participation in shaping collective political decisions. As for the second criticism, however, it is obviously vital to my study that the concept of citizenship should not limit the solidaristic community. After all, my intention is ultimately to show that global civil disobedience practices facilitate an international community of solidarity.

To be sure, the idea of an international community of solidarity remains dependent on national communities of citizens or peoples. After all, as I have argued all along, peoples organized into states retain normative priority as the primary source of responsibility taking in negotiating the reform of piecewise just or unfair terms of cooperation, in the global system. Nevertheless, the political goal is to create solidarity relations between decent peoples, as well as in their relations of such peoples to persons regardless of citizenship. To this extent, it is helpful to define solidarity instead as a type of *action*, working with others for a common political aim (Kolers 2012). This has the considerable virtue of detaching solidarity from nationality. Hence, anti-globalization activists in New York might work towards the common aim of resisting corporate globalization with fellow activists they have never met in Cochabamba protesting water privatization. Indeed, such activist may function as cosmopolitan citizens addressing a global public that includes other activists worldwide, but ultimately addresses the community of peoples responsible for negotiating international law concerning water right that are fair to a vulnerable and powerless sub-national community.

Here, mediated by the campaigns of diverse cosmopolitan citizens, solidarity between non-nationals need not entail any strong sense of reciprocity between those working together for a common political aim. Working together for the common political aim of motivating international uptake and reconsideration need not entail that the activists in Cochabamba should even be aware of the efforts made by the activists in New York (Rippe 1998; Harvey 2007). In this respect, the solidarity relation may be motivated in rather a one-sided way. It is sufficient for the development of such a relation that the New York activists should identify a condition – being a victim of corporate globalization and unfair terms of international cooperation – that makes those who suffer worthy of one's moral concern (Arnsperger and Varoufakis 2003). That said, however, the one-sidedness of the relationship in this latter definition of political solidarity points to the role of moral deference to the victims of injustice (Thomas 1993). Indeed, political solidarity entails an obligation of those more fortunate persons and peoples who have identified a condition of vulnerability to take appropriate action on behalf of those in a less favorable position within the global system.

Hence, political solidarity does not require a culturally specific account of the good life, proximity, or any strong sense of reciprocity between those participating in the solidarity relation. It is sufficient that a solidarity relation should identify those *in a condition of suffering, as the victims of injustices worthy of moral consideration*, wherever they are in the world. Such conditions of suffering and vulnerability are identified by cosmopolitan citizen disobedients, highlighting them to a global public and calling for uptake and reconsideration in the name of decency. Global civil disobedience practices thus clearly express global solidarity relations. This emerges most clearly in the idea from Chap. 5 of cosmopolitan disobedients taking a *morally deferential perspective of concern* for the most vulnerable in the context of global economic inequities. As noted in the introduction to this chapter, however, a similarly deferential perspective of concern and solidarity is expressed through assisted disobedience on behalf of the undocumented, and the conflicting perspectives of concern for the survival of decent peoples variously expressed by executives and disclosers. Indeed, in each case, different kinds of resort to extra-legality are appropriate expressions of moral deference and political solidarity.

Overall, I contend that political solidarity relations are the proper *goal* of diverse global civil disobedience practices by cosmopolitan citizens. This is consistent with Rawls' account of the goal of state-centered civil disobedience in *Theory* (1971), as the stabilization and ordering of social cooperation according to principles of justice. After all, as discussed here, political solidarity is an idea of orderliness, in the Rawlsian sense. It cannot be expected that those subject to unfair terms of cooperation will acquiesce indefinitely (Ibid) to their own exploitation and domination. The stability and order of the international community demands fair terms of cooperation, as embodying global political solidarity.

I turn now to an analytic redefinition of justifiable civil disobedience by cosmopolitan citizens in a global perspective. This will entail a review and synthesis of the key claims concerning definition and justification from the earlier chapters of this book, before reaffirming global solidarity as the appropriate goal of such justifiable disobedience.

7.3 Redefining Civil Disobedience in a Global Perspective

I proceed straight to the following broad schematic redefinition. Civil disobedience in a global perspective is:

1. a conscientiously-motivated form of public address contrary to law,
2. aiming at a change of law or policy, whether domestic or international, where
3. the disobedients may be (a) members of the same co-national body (b) cosmopolitan citizens united by shared commitments to political principles or (c) nation states and peoples, either liberal or hierarchical,
4. guided and justified by political principles, which may be either liberal or hierarchical principles insofar as these are consistent with the shared commitments of the *Law of Peoples* to decency and human right.
5. Here, the appeal to decency is intended by disobedient cosmopolitan citizen to highlight the piecewise just character and unfair terms of global cooperation, calling for uptake and reconsideration by the global public, in the cases of the undocumented and global economic inequities; or

6. in the case disobedient disclosures of government secrets, it is intended by the disclosers to preserve the moral character and integrity of the people and the ends of government by taking a contrary view of the entailments of decency from government executives resorting to secretive uses of prerogative.
7. Indeed, appealing to decency, disobedient cosmopolitan citizens address a diverse global public comprising many different actors besides peoples and states (IGOs, IFOs, INGOs, etc.), but the latter remain the primary addressees to the extent they are the primary source of responsibility taking in the global system.
8. Such resort to civil disobedience by diverse cosmopolitan citizens is indeed *justified* because decency is a moral consideration capable of defeating the duty of participants in global cooperation to obey either domestic or international law;
9. in particular, as capable of defeating the duty to obey, decency is aligned with a broad understanding of non-domination, prescribing the rights of all persons and people to effectively access the rule of law through contestations and dissent.
10. Finally, the goal of civil disobedience in a global perspective by cosmopolitan citizens is to create global solidarity relations with all those persons and peoples vulnerable to domination, in a merely piecewise just or unfair global system, or vulnerable to fundamental existential threats to a stable and decent international order.

This broad schematic expands upon Rawls' account of civil disobedience from *Theory* (1971) by taking certain key ideas of state centered disobedience and applying them instead to *Law of Peoples* (2001). Indeed, diverse cosmopolitan citizens engage in disobedient public address aimed at changing law and policy. Nevertheless, they address a global public about fundamental unfairness in a global, as opposed to national, system of cooperation, in which decency substitutes for liberal principles of domestic social justice. This substitution of decency for liberal social justice is the central idea of this book. In the introductory chapter, I stated that liberalism holds no justificatory monopoly on civil disobedience. Consistent with *Law of Peoples*, I denied that unfairness in the terms of global cooperation is exclusively about violations of liberal principles concerning the equal freedom of individual persons. Global justice is not liberal social justice writ large. I based this rejection of liberalism's justificatory monopoly, in part, on Rawls' concern from *Law of Peoples* that liberal principles could not become the basis of global justice without contradicting the principle of liberal toleration for non-liberal points of view.

Nevertheless, my primary concern is *not* with toleration for non-liberal viewpoints, but showing that they can also make positive contributions to the advancement of global justice through global civil disobedience practices. That is, rejecting liberal principles, disobedient cosmopolitan citizens from non-liberal societies and disobedient non-liberal peoples may make such contributions through globally disobedient public address to the international community of all decent peoples. Non-liberal viewpoints may make positive contributions to global justice through coalitions with disobedient cosmopolitan citizens from liberal societies or with disobedient liberal peoples. Indeed, collaboration of this sort across both liberal and non-liberal conceptions of justice are possible to the extent international decency becomes the ground for disobedient public address. This, of course, presupposes that non-liberal viewpoints can indeed ground disobedience. Consequently, I supplement the above schematic for civil disobedience in a global perspective with a schematic for justifiable civil disobedience by the citizens of decent non-liberal hierarchical societies and hierarchical peoples

(a) The citizens of hierarchical societies and hierarchical peoples have a prima facie obligation to abide by terms of both domestic and international cooperation as long as these are consistent with decency and human rights.
(b) Nevertheless, when these terms of cooperation violate decency, hierarchical citizens and peoples may legitimately resort disobedient public address (consistent with (8) above stating that decency is a moral consideration overriding the duty to obey).
(c) In particular, disobedience by hierarchical citizens and peoples is justified by violations of decency *as prescribing effective access to the rule of law for all persons and peoples, guaranteeing non-domination via contestations and dissent* (as consistent with (9) above),
(d) where, aligned to international decency, non-domination emerges as a shared commitment of both liberal and decent hierarchical peoples.

This supplementary schematic supports my broad redefinition of civil disobedience, in a global perspective, by showing how liberal and non-liberal viewpoints may *jointly express the goal of global solidarity* in the three cases that are the basis of my study. Indeed, such a joint expression of solidarity across liberal and non-liberal viewpoints may be clarified by considering the kinds of reforms or entailments of decency as non-domination following from the preceding chapters on the undocumented, global economic inequities, and the conflictual relationship of prerogative and disclosure as both justifiable under the rubric of decency.

In the case of the undocumented, international decency prescribes a novel human right.

7.4 The Addition to the Minimal List of Human Rights in *Law of Peoples* of the Human Right to Be a Political Participant, Wherever One Is

Such a right of all persons everywhere captures the general sense of non-domination aligned with decency insofar as it guarantees for the undocumented a contestatory voice in shaping domestic law and policy, in either liberal-democratic or decent non-liberal hierarchical societies. Here, the undocumented do not lay claim to the equal civil and political rights of liberal citizenship. Neither do they lay claim to any of the stratified group memberships defining citizenship of a decent non-liberal hierarchical society. After all, the point of a human right to be a political participant, wherever you are, is that it functions as a right of contestation and dissent *independent or freestanding* of any claims of exclusive national citizenship and territorial jurisdiction. It functions as such to the extent that decency prescribes that all peoples owe uptake and reconsideration to all persons within their jurisdictions. In this context, decency is both independent of all particular national citizenship claims and itself a positive standard of external criticism regarding any claims of exclusive citizenship. While independent of the claims of citizenship, the human right to be a political participant, wherever one is, is also respectful of these claims insofar as it is used to call upon the body of citizens, or people, to give uptake and reconsideration. Indeed, as my discussion of the undocumented is intended to show, recognition by all peoples of such a political contestatory right – quite independent of national citizenship – is a requirement of non-domination, grounded in decency. To this extent, international decency provides the basis for a joint expression of solidarity among both liberal and non-liberal hierarchical peoples for the undocumented as especially vulnerable populations in the global system.

Contrary to the first case concerning the undocumented, the second case concerning global economic inequities does not prescribe any novel human right, as much as point to an entailment of the equal sovereign rights of peoples.

7.5 The Recognition and Acceptance Among the International Community of the Entailments of the Fair Value of Liberty Between Rich and Poor Peoples, as Prescribed by the *Law of Peoples*

Here, recognizing and accepting this entailment of decency, again, highlights its positive role in advancing the cause of global justice, without reference to the particular claims of national citizenship. A core tenet of the *Law of Peoples* is the equality of peoples as opposed to persons. Nevertheless, as I argued in Chap. 4, there is no *fair value* of liberty between rich and poor peoples in the present global system. The richest peoples of the world exercise an undue power and influence over the terms of global economic cooperation with the poorest. Such an unfair value of liberty in shaping the terms of cooperation amounts to the domination by the global rich of the global poor. It is domination, in this internationalist sense, not so much because poor peoples require a status under international law as sovereign and entitled to a right of national self-determination. Indeed, as peoples, they are already recognized as entitled to an equal sovereign liberty of self-determination. The problem is that poor peoples often cannot exercise their equal liberty to shape and influence the terms of global economic cooperation: in other words, their liberty does not have a fair value. They are thus de facto dominated, in the global system, to the extent they cannot effectively use their liberty to effectively contest the terms of cooperation, as deliberated and decided upon by the rich. Above all, this unfair value of liberty between rich and poor peoples *entails an obligation of decency* for rich peoples to reconsider their participation in global economic cooperation. Such an obligation of decency is independent of those particular obligations of liberal and decent non-liberal hierarchical peoples to their own citizens, based on their different conceptions of justice, and the human right of all persons to political participation, wherever they are. Consequently, decency functions, once more, as basis for joint expressions of solidarity among different peoples with the global poor as an analytically distinct category of especially vulnerable persons and peoples in global economic cooperation. (Here, I note that the category of the global poor may overlap the category of undocumented persons).

As for resort to extra-legality by executives and disclosers, this also points to an entailment of decency rather than the introduction of any novel human right, such as transparency.

7.6 The Recognition and Acceptance Among the International Community of the Entailments of Competing Valid Claims Based on Decency and the Ends of Government Made by Executives and Disclosers

To the extent it is owed by all decent peoples, such recognition and acceptance of competing valid claims is not exclusive to a particular view of citizenship rights, like the Fourth Amendment rights of US citizens. Instead, all decent peoples are bound to recognize such claims to the justifiability of prerogative and disclosure. Granting its independence from any particular claims of national citizenship and its potential to make its own positive contributions to global justice, decency nonetheless turns out to be ambivalent regarding its entailments in this case. Indeed, the discourse of decency between peoples necessarily embraces this inherent ambivalence of entailments in working out appropriate responses to those resorting to extra-legality in keeping national security secrets and those exposing these secrets. To this extent, decency proves adaptable to the extreme complexity of current global politics. Adaptable to such complexity, decency and non-domination remain aligned in the sense that executive and disclosers are both concerned with ensuring the existential survival of a decent society and its freedom from domination. That is, its freedom from domination by international terrorism or the lack of government transparency in its efforts to secure such freedom, respectively. Hence, decency and non-domination function, again, as the basis of joint expressions of solidarity among all decent peoples with all vulnerable in global cooperation to these albeit different but related risks.

Overall, I stress that, as conceived here, such joint expressions of solidarity between peoples are not simply expressions of *moral* solidarity over the satisfaction of minimal humanitarian standards. In other words, they are not merely expressions of solidarity over the satisfaction of basic human needs and interests, conceived independently of political participation rights as extended to the most vulnerable populations in global cooperation. Indeed, consistent with my discussion in the first section of this chapter, solidarity is ultimately a political goal of creating a stable system of cooperation ordered by shared political principles. While employing different strategies, resort to disobedience facilitates this distinctively political goal in all three of the cases in my study. It does so to the extent that disobedients seek an orderly and stable global system by virtue of ensuring that marginalized and vulnerable persons and peoples gain effective access to the (domestic or international) rule of law and the possibility of positively shaping systemic reform.

Here, the disobedience strategy remains, above all, *discursive*. Solidarity is created not by the advocacy of particular policy reforms (concerning border controls, trade rules, distribution schemes, and so on), but presenting a challenge to decent peoples to live up to their own avowed commitments to global justice.

In *Theory* (1971), Rawls contends that the goal of disobedients is to avert a dilemma of submission or resistance for those who suffer persistent and deliberative violations of liberal principles of social justice. Disobedients advance this goal by not only asking a liberal people whether it wishes to acknowledge a clear and substantial violation of justice, but also reminding the people that it is unrealistic to expect those who face this dilemma to acquiesce indefinitely in their own domination or subordination. Indeed, on the one hand, disobedients invite the people to consider the unfairness of leaving the victims of a disordered system in the position of having to choose between submission and resistance. Nevertheless, on the other hand, they deliver not so much a threat (Rawls 1971) to the people as a 'reality check' concerning the ongoing stability of a system fundamentally disordered from the standpoint of justice. Here, disobedients place the onus on the people to respond by discursively assessing their obligations and responsibilities concerning the prospects for civic justice and social stability. The claim I make in this book is essentially the same one, adjusted to the global domain of politics. That is, civil disobedience in a global perspective places the onus on the international community of peoples to enter a global discourse over its obligations and responsibilities concerning global justice and global peace. This is the hitherto unexamined possibility of justifiable disobedience opened up by *Law of Peoples* (2001) with which I began in the introduction to this book.

To be sure, decency tempered with a pragmatic regard for the long-term consequences of leaving unfair terms of cooperation unaddressed ought to be sufficient to motivate a global discourse absent resort to disobedience. After all, decent peoples ought to give uptake to any claims regarding clear and substantial unfairness in global system. That is, they ought to be given uptake and reconsideration without the necessity for resort to disobedience. Nevertheless, civil disobedience becomes a justifiable option when uptake and reconsideration from those who are in a position to enact reform or revise unfair law or policy *is not forthcoming*. This is very clearly the case with respect to the undocumented, global economic inequities, and conscientious disclosers, insofar as controversy all too often deadlocks and stalls discourse. To be sure, the cases I have chosen for this book are not exhaustive of the possible justifiable uses of civil disobedience in a global perspective. For instance, further cases might include 'climate disobedience' or a range of other forms of environmental disobedience. Typically, advocates for environmental disobedience eschew the Rawlsian framework for civil disobedience I have employed (Welchman 2002; von Essen 2017). In large part, this is motivated by their resistance to the idea that environmental degradation is properly analyzed in terms of the urgent rights of humanity.

Nevertheless, solidarity relations with both vulnerable human and non-human animal populations are entirely feasible (von Essen and Allen 2017). Moreover, based on moral deference for the especially vulnerable, proxy contestations on behalf of non-human victims of environmental harms is broadly consisted with the analytical framework for civil disobedience in a global perspective that I have already developed. Moral deference and proxy contestations would even retain a connection to non-domination in human solidarity with non-human populations (Allen and von Essen 2016). In addition, given a global system in which peoples and states retain normative priority for deliberating and rectifying injustice and unfairness, disobedience expressing solidary with both human and non-human victims, say, of human caused climate change will still have to address the international community of peoples. Taking a perspective of concern for all life on the planet, environmental disobedience might overcome deliberation deficits by stimulating recommitment to the international Paris Accords (for a Rawlsian approach to climate justice, see Hauseby 2013). In these respects, environmental disobedience can be brought into alignment with my adapted Rawlsian framework, emphasizing moral deference and political solidarity concerning diverse populations rendered vulnerable in global cooperation, along with the centrality of peoples and states.

7.7 Conclusion

I began this book acknowledging that there has always been an internationalist dimension to civil disobedience. This is evident from the historical examples of Thoreau and Gandhi who resorted to disobedience primarily as a response to imperialism. My concern with disobedience in a global perspective, however, is not with imperialism as much as globalization. I understand globalization as different from imperialism to the extent that the former aspires to improve the prospects and opportunities of all persons and peoples through an integrated system of global cooperation. Indeed, as Rawls openly acknowledges in *Law of Peoples*, globalization is potentially intolerant of non-liberal viewpoints. Its harshest critics, however, also present globalization as another form of imperialism. Hence, globalization has become a new form of global imperial expansion whereby rich and powerful states seek to dominate substantial parts of the world for reasons of national economic gain and international political aggrandizement. This criticism is not without merit, given the merely piecewise just character of global cooperation, enabling co-nationals to dominate the undocumented, the global rich to dominate the global poor, and so on. Indeed, such a criticism presupposes – and I believe quite correctly – that globalization has not resulted in the death of the state.

Undoubtedly, globalization has been facilitated, in large part, by the post-World War II multiplication of agencies and authorities beyond the state: IGOs, IFOs, etc. Nevertheless, persistent structures of domination with globalization are very clearly functions of particular states using their superior power, influence, and resources to shape global cooperation in their national self-interest. If this analysis is correct and unequal state power continues to be a primary cause of merely piecewise justice and unfairness in the present system of global cooperation, then Rawls' key distinction from *Law of Peoples* between states and the peoples to whom they are accountable becomes highly relevant to advancing global justice. Indeed, as defined by their moral character and their commitments to decency and human rights, *peoples as distinct from the states they authorize* aspire to be *fair* to all participants in global cooperation. In other words, decent peoples aspire to fair terms of global cooperation, as an internationally shared ideal of relational global justice regulated by decency and human rights. To this extent, disobedient appeals by diverse cosmopolitan citizens to the moral character and conscience of peoples, in reassessing the fairness of international cooperation, offsets the potential for globalization to collapse into imperialism. It does so by calling upon decent peoples to redirect the uses of state power to non-strategic ends of global justice.

As motivated by disobedient public address, moral reassessment by decent peoples of the terms and entailments of fair cooperation between persons and peoples is thus a positive, non-violent way to facilitate global solidarity and stabilize current globalization processes. That is, it is a positive way to facilitate solidarity and stabilize such processes in a decent international order, appropriately tolerant of important variations in the moral characters of different peoples and their conceptions of justice. Indeed, in this final chapter, I have attempted to synthesize the discussions of the previous chapters by offering an analytical redefinition of civil disobedience in a global perspective. I have intended this redefinition to unpack the unexplored possibility of civil disobedience contained in *Law of Peoples*, with which I began this book. My hope is that by bringing clarity to its justification according to decency, as well as its goal of solidarity and stability, a global perspective on civil disobedience contributes to a realistically utopian outlook on contemporary global politics. Indeed, Rawls presents his vision of a decent international community in the *Law of Peoples* as a realistic utopia that neither under- nor over-plays the prospects for worldwide civility and justice.

On the one hand, the strategic amoralism of states in the old Westphalian world order underplays these prospects. On the other hand, over-ambitious projects of global justice as liberal social justice writ large risk overplaying them, at the not inconsiderable cost of violating toleration for non-liberal viewpoints and respect for the autonomy of those who subscribe to their prescriptions within the common parameters of decency. Here, decency is consistent with the future prospect for global justice clearly favored by Rawls himself of an historical transition to global commitments to liberal social justice principles *over time* (2001). It is consistent with this long term prospect insofar as decency prescribes uptake for constestations and dissent *across* both liberal and non-liberal viewpoints. Consequently, decency holds open the possibility of transitions from non-liberal to liberal conceptions of justice, as a matter of internal, domestic reform. Nevertheless, I have stressed throughout not the possibility of this internal transition, but rather the positive contribution of diverse cosmopolitan citizen appealing to decency in motivating reconsideration of fairness in the global system.

References

Allen, Michael P., and Erica Von Essen. 2016. Neo-Republicanism as a Route to Animal Non-Domination. *Politics and Animals* 2(1): 15–24.

Arnsperger, Christian, and Yanis Varoufakis. 2003. Towards a Theory of Solidarity. *Erkenntnis* 59(2): 157–188.

Beitz, Charles. 2011. *The Idea of Human Rights*. Oxford: Oxford University Press.

Brownlee, Kimberlee. 2012. *Conscience and Conviction: The Case for Civil Disobedience*. Oxford: Oxford University Press.

Harvey, Jean. 2007. Moral Solidarity and Empathetic Understanding: The Moral Value and Scope of the Relationship. *Journal of Social Philosophy* 38(1): 22–37.

Hauseby, Robert. 2013. *Rawls and Climate Justice: An Amendment to the Law of Peoples*. *Environmental Ethics* 35(2): 227–243.

Kolers, Avery. 2012. Dynamics of Solidarity. *Journal of Political Philosophy* 20(4): 137–156.

Krishnamurthy, Meena. 2013. Political Solidarity, Justice and Public Health. *Public Health Ethics* 6(2): 129–141.

Lenard, Patti, Christine Straehle, and Lea Ypi. 2010. Global Solidarity. *Contemporary Political Theory* 9(1): 99.

Miller, David. 2012. *National Responsibility and Global Justice*. Oxford: Oxford University Press.
Nagel, Thomas. 2005. The Problem of Global Justice. *Philosophy and Public Affairs* 33(2): 113–147.
Rawls, John. 2001. *The Law of Peoples*. Cambridge, MA: Harvard University Press.
———. 1971. *A Theory of Justice*. Cambridge, MA: Harvard University Press.
Rehg, Willian. 1997. *Insight and Solidarity: The Discourse Ethics of Jürgen Habermas, Philosophy, Social Theory, and the Rule of Law*. Berkeley: University of California Press.
Rippe, Klause. 1998. Diminishing Solidarity. *Ethical Theory and Moral Practice* 1(3): 355–373.
Sandel, Michael. 1997. *Democracy's Discontent: America in Search of a Public Philosphy*. Cambridge, MA: Belknap.
Straehle, Christine. 2010. National and Cosmopolitan Solidarity. *Contemporary Political Theory* 9(1): 110–120.
Thomas, Laurence. 1993. Moral Flourishing in an Unjust World. *Journal of Moral Education* 22(2): 83–96.
von Essen, Erica. 2017. Environmental Disobedience and the Dialogic Dimension of Dissent. *Democratization* 24(2): 305–324.
Von Essen, Erica and Michael P. Allen. 2017. *Solidarity Between Human and Non-Human Animals: Representing Animal Voices in Policy Deliberations*. doi 10.1080/17524032.1269820.
Welchman, Jennifer. 2001. Is Ecosabotage Civil Disobedience? *Philosophy and Geography* 4(1): 97–107.

The manufacturer's authorised representative in the EU is Springer Nature Customer Service Centre GmbH, Europaplatz 3, 69115 Heidelberg, Germany. If you have any concerns regarding our products, please contact ProductSafety@springernature.com

Printed and bound by CPI Group (UK) Ltd, Croydon, CR0 4YY
25/09/2026
02222898-0018